SOMEONE CARED

Prose and Prayers Inspired by the Poetry of John Gowans

by Rob Birks

SOMEONE CARED
Rob Birks
2014 Frontier Press

Birks, Rob
SOMEONE CARED

December 2014

Scripture references used in this text are from The Holy Bible, New International Version, New Living Translation, New American Standard, Amplified Bible, The Living Bible.

THE HOLY BIBLE, NEW INTERNATIONAL VERSION®, NIV® Copyright © 1973, 1978, 1984, 2011 by Biblica, Inc.™ Used by permission. All rights reserved worldwide.

The King James Version is public domain in the United States.

Scripture taken from The Message. Copyright © 1993, 1994, 1995, 1996, 2000, 2001, 2002. Used by permission of NavPress Publishing Group.

ISBN 978-0-9908776-1-5

Printed in the United States

For Stacy

Sharing poetry introduced our hearts to each other.
I couldn't be more grateful.

I love you more than dreams and poetry.
More than laughter, more than tears, more than mystery.
I love you more than rhythm, more than song
I love you more with every breath I draw.
—T Bone Burnett

There is nothing quite like walking through an art gallery with a docent, or the curator himself. This is the feeling I get as I read Major Robert Birks' beautiful unveiling of the poetry of John Gowans. He is an informed, inspired guide whose joy regarding the poet's work is contagious. With the backdrop of The Salvation Army's century and a half of service to the world's poor, these songs and reflections are born of meaningful engagement with a living gospel.

—Sara Groves
Singer/Songwriter

This book has the audacity to intertwine the moving verses of John Gowans, the author's own personal experiences and spiritual discoveries, the testimony of Scripture, a rich sampling of pop songs, biographies and news events—expecting, unrealistically, that such juxtaposing will somehow result in a coherent outcome and a deeper and more incisive understanding of spiritual reality. I am startled to say Rob succeeds. *Someone Cared* is a meditation on the gifted poetry of John Gowans well worth savoring and a journey definitely worth taking.

—Commissioner Phil Needham
Author of *When God Becomes Small*

Rob Birks has done us all a favor in bringing to our attention again the poetry and writing of John Gowans. Of both Rob and John the words of the psalmist apply: *Beautiful words stir my heart. I will recite a lovely poem about the king, for my tongue is like the pen of a skillful poet* (Ps. 45:1 NLT).

—Colonel Janet Munn, Training Principal,
School for Officer Training
The Salvation Army Australia Eastern Territory
Co-Author of *Army On Its Knees*:
The Dynamics of Great Commission Prayer

Poetry distills truth as it entices the heart and enlightens the mind. The poet generates a deeper and fuller understanding of the reality it ponders. In his volume of devotional prose and prayers, Rob Birks skillfully employs the resplendent poetry of John Gowans as the basis for reflection on the many facets of God's amazing love and abundant provision. The result is a remarkable infusion of new light and life flowing from the vibrant, insightful words of the master poet. Appealing equally to heart and mind, *Someone*

Cared is adaptable for personal reflection as well as group discussion. I highly recommend it.

—Commissioner William W. Francis
Author of *The Stones Cry Out, Celebrate the Feasts of the Lord* and
Building Blocks of Spiritual Leadership

Rob Birks' writings on the Poet Generals of The Salvation Army—Albert Orsborn and John Gowans—are simultaneously inspiring and whimsical, a challenge to the community of faith and an entertaining romp. As in ORS**BORN**AGAIN: *A New Look at Old Songs of New Life* (2013), Birks' meditations on the writings of The Salvation Army's sixteenth General combines engaging insights with an ease of communication that is both inviting and disarming. Finding wisdom in the most diverse places—everything from Bob Dylan to *The Princess Bride* to the evening news—the reflections in *Someone Cared: Prose and Prayers Inspired by the Poetry of John Gowans* are sure to bring comfort to the soul and a smile to the face.

—Michael J. Gilmour, Providence University College
Author of *The Gospel According to Bob Dylan: The Old, Old Story for Modern Times* and *Eden's Other Residents: The Bible and Animals*

Someone Cared is a beautiful compilation of poetry, Scripture, spiritual reflections, and humor. Reading this book feels like reconnecting with a good friend. Gowans' tender lyrics matched with Rob Birks' honest reflections caused a stirring in my soul. The pages of this book are filled with powerful glimpses of God's grace and overwhelming goodness. Ultimately readers will be inspired by the incredible truth that life is beautiful because Someone Cared.

—Trina Pockett, Speaker, Writer, & Friend
trinapockett.com

Let's be clear. Melodies are what I do. Chord progressions, all day long. Sounds and noise are my language. Words? Words are hard. I've reconciled this in my heart. John Gowans, however, is hands-down one of the most prolific wordsmiths in The Salvation Army's hymnody (and history). How he so cleverly and articulately could thread one golden idea after another into poetry and prose is utterly beyond me. Be it the beautiful depiction of heaven's gathering in "They Shall Come From The East" or the heart-wrenching boldness, pleading the Spirit in "His Provision," his pen has created many wordscapes that have affected believers across the globe. Equally as astounding and alluring, Rob Birks' telling and retelling of these gems, through a gift that is uniquely his, reminds us (Salvos or not) that there is power in the word. And in the Word. You will not be disappointed with my challenge to you: Read this book. Then try to prove me wrong.

—Marty Mikles
Atlanta, Georgia
transMission.virb.com

Jesus said, *"Come to me all who are weary and heavy-laden and I will give you rest"* (Matt. 11:28 NAS). *Someone Cared* is a faithful companion on the journey to soul rest. Its rhythm and cadence brings hope. Its words brings life, and its message brings truth. Each Gowans lyric, with accompanying harmonies by Birks, saturates the burdened heart, calling us to come as we are into the embracing arms of our Savior. In Christ and Christ alone we find the ability to sing anew, and the opportunity to find rest, rest for our souls.

—Craig Bowler, Pastor
Sanctuary
Kennesaw, Georgia

Rob Birks doesn't catch our attention by chance, but by design. In this case, his design is to ensure we know that someone cares deeply about you and me. Saddling the poetic words of John Gowans with devotional thought and a propensity for clever prose, Birks will capture your attention in *Someone Cared*—and you will be glad he did.

—Christin Davis
Managing Editor
New Frontier Publications

Keep me safe, my God, for in you I take refuge. I say to the Lord, "You are my Lord; apart from you I have no good thing." I say of the holy people who are in the land, "They are the noble ones in whom is all my delight" (Ps. 16:1-3).

When we need someone or someplace to take refuge in, we find the safest spot in God alone. However, once we are located in the refuge that is God, we not only find the Spirit there, but we find others like us seeking refuge. And some of them are "saints"—"holy people who are in the land … noble ones"—in whom we get to delight! When we think about these people (some of whom have gone on to the next phase of life before us) we find the fullness of their lives naturally spilling over into ours. What Rob Birks has done in this wonderful book is help us "delight" in one of the "noble ones" from The Salvation Army's recent history. Thank you for letting some of us unfamiliar with John Gowans and his amazing repository of poems and songs get our first glimpse of this "noble one." In feasting on his life and writings I am sure any reader will find great delight.

—Rev. Bart Tarman

DNA connects families in the same way it connects poets, songwriters and lyricists. This group sees things through different artistic eyes; they take some words, sort them in a grand order to string a lovely sentence with rhythm and we hear this rhythm through their ears. King David, King Solomon, Robbie Burns, Hoagy Carmichael, Albert Orsborn and John Gowans were magnificent word sorters. They could see an old bridge and make something out of it, as did John Gowans in his poem about becoming a strong spiritual bridge in the second devotional. Rob Birks is added to this list. He has the innate ability to sort words into inspirational sentences, which then awake our souls to new and worshipful praise. I believe *Someone Cared* will bless you as it has me.

—Barbara Newbould, Friend
Follower of Jesus for over 75 years

As a pastor I often preach how important prayer and reflection are for nurture and growth in the life of faith. Yet, if the truth be told, I have shelves of devotional books that I had all the best intentions to use but they have yet to be read. I wish I had known of the poems of John Gowans, because they wouldn't have stayed on my shelf for long. Robert Birks' insight and reflection in *Someone Cared* made Gowans' words come alive to me, like fresh water to a tired soul.

—Rev. Maggi Henderson
Old First Presbyterian Church
San Francisco, California
Board Chair—San Francisco Interfaith Council

TABLE OF CONTENTS

FOREWORD

In the mid-1800s William and Catherine Booth took to the streets of London armed with a story. It was an old story from the ancient Near East retold for the thieves, prostitutes, gamblers, and drunkards working the streets of London's East End. The main character in the story was Jesus of Nazareth, son of Mary, friend to sinners. The plot? Someone cares. Namely God. Team Booth gave their story project a name, The Salvation Army. And what an army it has become. The world over, The Salvation Army is known for the story that saves from the God who cares. But that's not all. To be truly understood, saving care must be embodied. Prison ministry, disaster relief, help for the homeless, and the combating of human trafficking are just a few ways that The Salvation Army makes saving care visible.

Today, relief agencies, NGOs, and mercy ministries are everywhere and in everything. Many of my music business concerns are linked to non-profit caring of some variety, from the Grammy's MusicCares program to Blood:Water Mission here in Nashville. Much has been made of our Nashville music community and its role in advocating for Africa and using our celebrity platforms for redemptive storytelling. From a political standpoint, our loud voices have made a difference. On July 2, 2011, I was backstage with ONE Campaign founder Bono from U2. We connected again on what drew us together in the first place—the old story about someone caring. "That really changed things, that was a pivotal moment," he said, referring to a meeting he led at our home—the Art House in Nashville—in December 2002. So what happened? Unfortunately, more than I can tell. But at the very least, a prophet dressed up as a rock star riffed on 2,000-year-old ancient Near East words like, *"Do unto others as you would have them do to you"* (Luke 6:31). Jesus says that.

No disrespect to the famous Irishman above, but the real pioneers in this linking of care and music, the real rock stars, are found in The Salvation Army. One such star, in a long trajectory of bright lights, is Rob Birks. I've known the major/general secretary of the Golden State Division for almost 30 years. I proudly claim him as a superfan of my music and the music I produce for others. Rob has dedicated his life to telling the story that there is someone who cares. Rather than draw attention to himself though, he wants his readers to drink in the inspiration and wisdom of one of The Salvation Army's great musical stars from the past, John Gowans. Like Rob and Bono today, John Gowans was about the care and the music. Not only did he lead the worldwide movement from 1999 to 2002, he contributed greatly to The Salvation Army musical canon. He was a major dude and caring poet.

Step into history, into a long story of words for the common good. Quiet yourself. Breathe. Read. Have ears to hear and eyes to see. Then pray and hit the streets. The story is not over. There's more poetry to write, more songs to sing.

CHARLIE PEACOCK,
Music Producer/Recording Artist
Nashville, Tennessee
June 21, 2014

INTRODUCTION

In my former book, Theophilus …. Wait, that doesn't sound right. I don't know anyone named Theophilus, nor have I ever written a book entitled *Theophilus*. May the author begin the book by humbly asking the reader for the grace to begin again?

In my former book, *ORSBORNAGAIN*, I considered the poetry of Albert Orsborn, the sixth General (international leader) of The Salvation Army, a part of the universal Christian Church. Throughout the book I referred to Orsborn as the first Poet General. That's because The Salvation Army has had (at least) two international leaders who were well versed in the art of poetry. The second Poet General was John Gowans, who led our worldwide movement from 1999 to 2002. Gowans was prolific, writing three *O Lord* books of prayer poems, an autobiography entitled *There's A Boy Here*, and co-writing 10 musicals in 23 years (1967-1990) with his friend General John Larsson. The songwriting team of Gowans and Larsson is legendary in The Salvation Army (think Rodgers and Hammerstein, or Lennon and McCartney, or Elton John and Bernie Taupin, or Jimmy Jam and Terry Lewis, or Macklemore and Ryan Lewis, depending on your age or musical taste). Nineteen Gowans and Larsson songs are in the current version of The Salvation Army Song Book (hymnal).

Gowans was a childhood hero of mine. His look, his style, his voice, his work—he was the real deal in my eyes, personable, posh and poetic. For *Someone Cared*, I allowed his songs and poems to inspire devotional pieces which, Lord willing, will inspire the reader to embrace and emulate the vast love of God. I am of the opinion that the unmerited, unconditional and unending love of God serves as the overall theme for the life work of John Gowans. That God loves everyone and has everyone's best interest at heart may seem like lightweight stuff, professed by people who are too naïve to know anything of the weightier issues people face. On the contrary, authentic Jesus followers know that life can be rough and believe that the boundless love of God is strong enough to cling to through terrible and tragic times. To experience those times without the belief that God loves us would be unbearable. In her book of essays, *When I Was a Child I Read Books*, Pulitzer Prize-winning author Marilynne Robinson wrote, "I experience religious dread whenever I find myself thinking that I know the limits of God's grace, since I am utterly certain it exceeds any imagination a human being might have of it. God does, after all, so love the world." Brilliant!

Gowans was keenly aware that millions of people live their lives in a constant state of "religious dread," thinking that God—if there even is a God—cannot or will not or must not love them. So, he wrote love songs. His most popular in Salvation Army circles is, arguably, "Someone Cares," which begins with the lyric: "Do you sometimes feel that no one truly knows you, and that no one understands or really cares?" The answer? Someone cares! The same Someone that Marilynne Robinson wrote of.

I am so thankful that John Gowans also cared. He cared enough to contemplate and communicate the love of God, a love that is for everyone, whether they care or couldn't care less. Sadly (for us, not for him), General John Gowans died in December of 2012. However, he left a legacy of lyrics and willed his words to all who would enter into and enjoy them. Here's praying you are able to do both.

Someone Cares

Do you sometimes feel that no one truly knows you,
And that no one understands or really cares?
Through his people, God himself is close beside you,
And through them he plans to answer all your prayers.

Someone cares, someone cares,
Someone knows your deepest need, your burden shares;
Someone cares, someone cares,
God himself will hear the whisper of your prayers.

Ours is not a distant God, remote, unfeeling,
Who is careless of our loneliness and pain,
Through the ministry of men he gives his healing,
In their dedicated hands brings hope again.

John Gowans

"When you care enough to send the very best." So goes the old advertising slogan of a well-known greeting card company. Whether or not they are the very best is debatable, I suppose. For the sake of argument, let's say they are. Does it necessarily follow that sending one of their cards to someone is clear cut proof that you care for that someone? Again, debatable.

"Long distance is the next best thing to being there," is another (also dated) advertising slogan from a telecommunications corporation. The commercials (back in the day) for their long distance service depicted all kinds of people describing their desire to share something special with a loved one: good news, new birth, an urgent message, and so on.

Both of these slogans were brilliant marketing campaigns because almost everyone has experienced a time, or several times, when someone they cared for was far away, and being near that person was impossible. In these cases, a card or a call is all we are left with (or *were* left with, pre-Skype, texting, Facebook, Twitter, Instagram, et al.) to convey our love and care for someone. The card may or may not be the very best we can send, but it can mean so much to someone. And while long distance or another, more modern form of communication is definitely not as good as being there, hearing the voice of someone who cares for you can bring joy, peace and healing.

In the song "Someone Cares," John Gowans is writing to a person who feels desperately distant from someone—a person who needs the very best sent to them. He is writing to the person (you?) who sometimes feels that no one truly knows, understands or cares for him. He is writing to the person (someone you care for?) who misunderstands God as being remote and unfeeling. He is writing to the person (someone who cares for you?) who wonders if God couldn't care less about her loneliness and pain. He is writing to someone whose experience is similar to that of the psalmist: *Look and see, there is no one at my right hand; no one is concerned for me. I have no refuge; no one cares for my life* (Ps. 142:4).

Yet, this song is packed with good news! Someone really cares! The creator of the universe cares about and for every living thing in the universe. He is close beside us. He knows our deepest need. He shares our burden (Ps. 55:22, 1 Pet. 5:7). He hears and answers our prayers. He brings hope and healing. Can you handle more good news? Yes? Okay, here goes. You and I get to be the answers to prayers. You and I get to give healing. You and I get to bring hope. It's not that God can't do all this without us (because he can). Rather, he allows the "dedicated hands" of "his people" to show how much he cares. It's a privileged partnership of prayer answering that he invites us into. Take a look at the people around you. Not now, maybe. Depending on where you are while you are reading this, there may not be anyone around you. But on your way to work, while you are in class, the next time you're at the gym (Note to self: Get to the gym.), look closely and care-fully at the people around you. Does anyone truly know them? Do you think there is anyone in their lives who understands them? Do they have someone who really cares? The answer to these three questions is a resounding YES! Some One does! And so should someone, or some two, or three, more.

PRAYER

O God, thank you for caring enough to send the very best in the person of Jesus Christ—your Son and our Savior—who did not let the long distance we created with our sin keep him from serving us, seeking us, saving us and sending his Spirit to work in and through us. May our love and care for OTHERS be the hallmark of our devotion to you. Amen.

A Tale of Four Bridges

I want to be a bridge,
Though I'm not strong.
I want to be a bridge
So wide, so long
That over me from doubt
To faith may pass
The lad in search of God,
The seeking lass.

Put steel into my faith
And concrete too,
That men may travel
Over me
To You!

John Gowans

The George Washington Bridge spans the Hudson River, allowing vehicles to travel between Fort Lee, New Jersey, and Manhattan. Construction on the bridge began in October 1927 and the bridge was dedicated on October 24, 1931. Approximately 102 million vehicles cross the bridge each year. On September 9, 2013, two of the bridge's toll lanes were closed, causing a huge traffic jam that affected thousands in Fort Lee and the surrounding communities. So far, so normal, right? Stuff happens. Lanes close. Traffic jams. What makes these lane closures and this traffic jam unusual is the fact that people intentionally caused it all to happen. The exact details are still coming out (some never will, most likely), but what seems to be clear is that members of New Jersey Governor Chris Christie's staff ordered the lane closures as payback directed at the Fort Lee mayor, who did not support Christie's run for reelection. As of yet, no one knows whether or not "Bridgegate" will close down the governor's chances for a presidential run.

The Edmund Pettus Bridge was built in 1940 and crosses the Alabama River in Selma, Alabama. March 7, 1965, was the date of the first of three civil rights marches to protest the exclusion of black Americans from the voting process. The marchers were headed to the capital city of Montgomery, but were stopped and attacked by state and local police after crossing the bridge. Scenes of the tragic event, now known as Bloody Sunday, were broadcast on television. Like most attempts to crush the truth, what happened at the end of the Edmund Pettus Bridge highlighted a horrible injustice, and gave momentum to the Selma Voting Rights Movement.

The Bridge School is located in Hillsborough, California, 20 minutes from where I currently live. It was founded in 1986, and it exists to help children with complex communication needs. Its mission statement reads in part, "The Bridge School is a non-profit organization whose mission is to ensure that individuals with severe speech and physical impairments achieve full participation in their communities." One of the founders of the Bridge School is Pegi Young. Pegi's husband is Neil, as in Neil Young, as in Crosby, Stills, Nash & Young, as in Neil Young and Crazy Horse, as in "searching for a heart of gold" Neil Young, as in 1996 Rock and Roll Hall of Fame inductee Neil Young. Anyway, Pegi and Neil have a son, Ben, who was born with cerebral palsy. When her search for an educational institution equipped to meet Ben's needs ended in disappointment, Pegi joined forces with another parent and a doctor to form the Bridge School. Each year, Neil calls some of his musician friends, asking them to join him for the Bridge School Benefit, with all proceeds going to the school. Unfortunately, over the last 27 years, not too many famous musicians have answered the call. Unless you consider these musicians famous: Bruce Springsteen, Bob Dylan, James Taylor, Elvis Costello, Elton John, Bonnie Raitt, Simon and Garfunkel, Emmylou Harris, Tony Bennett, Paul McCartney, and Arcade Fire (just to name a few). Okay, maybe they are famous. And they answered the compelling call from their famous friend to help his not-so-famous son and thousands of not-so-famous OTHERS.

The fourth bridge is you. The fourth bridge is me. What kind of bridge are we?

Are we known for our traffic jams, caused to make someone pay for a perceived injustice against us? Are we going against our design and purpose, simply to settle some score? Is there a blockade at one end of our bridge protecting a prejudice? Are we infamous for the aggressive actions we support, or famous for our freedom fighting? Can those with needs to be met find in us a safe place? Is our mission so critical and appealing that others are lining up, answering the call to join in?

Is our foundation strong enough to support those "in search of God" as they cross over "from doubt to faith?" Are we helping or hindering OTHERS from making their way to Jesus?

"Greater love has no one than this: to lay down one's life for one's friends" (John 15:13).

When times get rough and friends just can't be found
Like a bridge over troubled water I will lay me down.
—Paul Simon ("Bridge over Troubled Water")

Triumph and Rest

They shall come from the east,
they shall come from the west,
And sit down in the Kingdom of God;
Both the rich and the poor,
The despised, the distressed,
They'll sit down in the kingdom of God.
And none will ask what they have been
Provided that their robes are clean;
They shall come from the east,
they shall come from the west,
And sit down in the Kingdom of God.

They shall come from the east,
they shall come from the west,
And sit down in the Kingdom of God.
To be met by their Father and welcomed and blessed,
And sit down in the Kingdom of God.
The black, the white, the dark, the fair,
Your color will not matter there;
They shall come from the east,
they shall come from the west,
And sit down in the Kingdom of God.

They shall come from the east,
they shall come from the west,
And sit down in the Kingdom of God.
Out of great tribulation to triumph and rest
They'll sit down in the Kingdom of God.
From every tribe and every race,

All men as brothers shall embrace;
They shall come from the east,
they shall come from the west,
And sit down in the Kingdom of God.

John Gowans

As I write, it's game on for the XXII Winter Olympics. Over 2,800 athletes from 88 nations have traveled to Sochi, Russia, to compete in 98 events. There was much controversy before the games began (security, the host country's anti-LGBT laws, terrorist threats, faulty hotel plumbing, etc.) but the moment 11-year-old Liza Temnikova appeared on stage to lead the world through the opening ceremonies in the Fisht Olympic Stadium, those controversies were put on ice, in favor of what was going to take place on the ice and on the slopes over the next few weeks.

By the time you read this, the games will have been completed, and we will all know who won the gold, silver and bronze medals in each event. The Olympic Village will be empty, since the athletes will have traveled back to their homelands as heroes and heroines. NBC will go back to its regularly scheduled programs, and many countries will go back to their pre-Olympic modus operandi of distrust and vilify. For now, though, grace has the edge over grudges, athleticism overtakes animosity, and one's podium placement far outweighs one's political philosophy. For me, the medal count is interesting, but it is not the most inspirational part of the Olympic Games. When the snowboarders at the bottom of the hill greet with open arms the snowboarder who just knocked them out of medal contention, that's what it's all about. Call me sentimental, but with Nick Lowe I ask,

"What's so funny 'bout peace, love and understanding?"

On this side of the finish line, we only see this pageant of peace every two years. But there will come a day when nations will come together for an eternity of harmonious togetherness. And our eyes will be on the Prize.

In John's vision—recorded in Revelation, the last book of the Bible—there is a lot of crazy stuff happening that scholars and theologians and authors have struggled for 2,000 years to decipher. Some parts of the vision, however, seem simple. For instance, in the seventh chapter of Revelation, just after the 144,000 (whatever that really means) from all the tribes of Israel were sealed, John saw something spectacular:

> *After this I looked, and there before me was a great multitude that no one could count, from every nation, tribe, people and language, standing before the throne and before the Lamb. They were wearing white robes and were holding palm branches in their hands. And they cried out in a loud voice: "Salvation belongs to our God, who sits on the throne, and to the Lamb"* (Rev. 7:9-10).

A few verses later, we are told who the multitude is: *"These are they who have come out of the great tribulation; they have washed their robes and made them white in the blood of the Lamb"* (Rev. 7:14).

In case you aren't familiar with language like "blood of the Lamb," the Lamb is Jesus, who sacrificed his life to save ours by shedding his blood while dying in our place. As the apostle Paul wrote in his letter to the Christians in Rome, *Work hard for sin your whole life and your pension is death. But God's gift is real life, eternal life, delivered by Jesus, our Master* (Rom. 6:23 MSG). So, the multitude in John's vision is made up of those from every nation, tribe, people and language. These are those who are clean, thanks to what Jesus

did when he died for them.
And now we see that he is still taking care of them:

> *"they are before the throne of God and serve him day and night in his temple; and he who sits on the throne will shelter them with his presence. 'Never again will they hunger; never again will they thirst. The sun will not beat down on them,' nor any scorching heat. For the Lamb at the center of the throne will be their shepherd; 'he will lead them to springs of living water. And God will wipe away every tear from their eyes'"* (Rev. 7:15-17).

There's no getting around it. The ice and snow of the XXII Winter Olympic Games will eventually melt, and cold wars may make a comeback. But for those all around the world who hunger and thirst, for those who come out of "great tribulation," there is "triumph and rest." And no one needs to work towards this prize. There is no effort to be made. All that is required is to accept the worldwide invitation for "every tribe and every race" to "sit down in the Kingdom of God." All expenses paid!

Pray Where You Are

What shall I ask for you,
What shall I pray?
Speaking to God for you,
What shall I say?
Shall I ask influence,
Shall I ask wealth?
Shall I ask happiness, harmony, health?

This I will ask for you: God grant each day,
Wisdom to know His will, grace to obey.
This I will ask for you: God grant each day,
Wisdom to know His will, grace to obey.
Wisdom to know His will, grace to obey.

If I could see for you
What lies ahead.
What you should greet with joy,
What you should dread;
I'd bridge the stream for you,
Fence every height,
Life would be beautiful, burdenless, bright;

What e're the future holds, This is my prayer:
God who is with you here be with you there!
What e're the future holds, This is my prayer:
God who is with you here be with you there!
God who is with you here be with you there!

John Gowans

I grew up on *Fiddler on the Roof* (and Lemonheads and *Mad* magazine and "Starsky & Hutch," but I digress). Long before we could own a copy of the film and watch it whenever we wished, our family enjoyed a long-standing "tradition" (cue dramatic Jerry Bock music) of watching this classic 1971 film together. Clocking in at just over three hours (without commercials), this tradition was not for the faint of heart. These were also the days before fast-forwarding through the slower parts was possible. It has become one of my favorite movies—right up there with *Citizen Kane* and *To Kill a Mockingbird*. Even as a kid, I loved this movie. Maybe my fascination with it has something to do with the fact that watching and singing along with it was a family affair. Maybe it's some strange kind of new math: I love my family + My family loves *Fiddler* = I love *Fiddler*. However, while I do love my family, my family loves tuna casserole and I certainly don't (Sorry, Mom.), so there goes that theory. There are so many things I love about this film: Tevye shaking it up while singing at the top of his lungs in the barn; the witty dialogue between Tevye and the townspeople; the cute crankiness of Yente the village matchmaker; the complicated relationship between Tevye and Golde, his wife; and a dream sequence that is at once humorous and haunting. But by far, what I love most about *Fiddler on the Roof* is the fact that throughout the film, Tevye is speaking with God. When he is thankful, he speaks with God. When he is angry, he speaks with God. When he is drunk, he speaks with God. Whether he's just heard good news or terrible news, he speaks with God.

One of those occurrences comes fairly early in the story. Preparations for the Sabbath have been made and the whole family is together, including the tailor, Motel Kamzoil, who later presents himself to Tevye as a son-in-law candidate, and ~~Starsky~~, I mean Perchik, who presents himself as a clear threat to tradition (and also as a son-in-law candidate). Before the meal, Golde and Tevye sing the "Sabbath Prayer" over their five daughters. Here is what they pray:

> May the Lord protect and defend you.
> May He always shield you from shame.
> May you come to be
> In Israel a shining name.
>
> May you be like Ruth and like Esther.
> May you be deserving of praise.
> Strengthen them, Oh Lord,
> And keep them from the strangers' ways.
>
> May God bless you and grant you long lives.
> (May the Lord fulfill our Sabbath prayer for you.)
> May God make you good mothers and wives.
> (May He send you husbands who will care for you.)
>
> May the Lord protect and defend you.
> May the Lord preserve you from pain.
> Favor them, Oh Lord, with happiness and peace.
> Oh, hear our Sabbath prayer. Amen.

I'm ashamed to admit that as a kid this was one of those boring parts I would've fast-forwarded through if the technology at the time had allowed. Now, having (nearly) raised three kids with the always gorgeous and ever-gracious Stacy, this has become one of the most important scenes for me.

I still watch *Fiddler*, usually over the holidays or when my oldest daughter, Emily, comes home from college. I'm trying to pass that tradition on to the next generation. Isn't that what parenthood is all about? Speaking of "Parenthood"

(Were we?), that's something I watch a little more of these days than I do *Fiddler*. I know, Berkeley, California, is a long way from Anatevka, Russia, but the Bravermans actually have several things in common with Tevye, Golde and their daughters. For instance, both families …. Okay, maybe not several things, but one thing is for sure: The parents of both fictional families love their children and want what's best for them.

The theme song for the NBC show was brilliantly chosen and perfectly describes the hopes and dreams Zeek and Camille (graduates of the 1960s) have for their four adult children. The song is Bob Dylan's "Forever Young." Written in the same spirit (Spirit?) as the "Sabbath Prayer" sung by Tevye and Golde, this classic speaks of the deep desire one can have that God's best be manifested in another. Truly this song is one of the best ever written. Here's the second verse:

> May you grow up to be righteous
> May you grow up to be true
> May you always know the truth
> And see the lights surrounding you
> May you always be courageous
> Stand upright and be strong
> May you stay forever young.

A few years before *Fiddler on the Roof* was filmed and before Dylan's "Forever Young" was written, John Gowans wrote the words we are considering here. The song made its debut in a musical called *Hosea*, a retelling of the Biblical prophet's true life role as an object lesson of God's unmerited, unconditional and unending love for his people. The poet begins his prayer in the same manner most of us begin ours: not knowing what to say. After briefly considering some possibilities in the first verse, he finally determines to pray simply for "Wisdom to know His will, grace to obey."

At the conclusion of the song, Gowans leaves us with the comforting truth found in Matthew 28:20 that God is omnipresent (everywhere at once) and promises always to be with us.

Is there someone in your life who needs your prayers today? Are the words hard to come by? Try borrowing a few from Gowans, or Dylan, or Tevye and Golde (lyrics by Sheldon Harnick). Or maybe even this prayer of John Calvin, excerpted from his *Commentary on Hosea*:

Grant, Almighty God, that as thou hast once appeared in the person of thy only-begotten Son, and hast rendered in him thy glory visible to us, and as thou dost daily set forth to us the same Christ in the glass of thy gospel,— O grant, that we, fixing our eyes on him, may not go astray, nor be led here and there after wicked inventions, the fallacies of Satan, and the allurements of this world: but may we continue firm in the obedience of faith and persevere in it through the whole course of our life, until we be at length fully transformed into the image of thy eternal glory, which now in part shines in us, through the same Christ our Lord. Amen.

Jesse Girl and the Light Fantastic

Hope, like a candle, cancels the darkness,
Flickering fragile flame.
Hope, like a lantern, outlives the darkness,
Always remains the same,
Always remains the same.

Hope, like the sunrise, chases the shadows.
Darkness resists in vain.
Nothing can crush it. Nothing can kill it.
Buried it lives again!
Buried it lives again!

Christ is The Candle. Christ is The Lantern.
Christ The Eternal Flame.
Christ is The Sunrise, Scatt'ring the shadows.
Buried He lives again!
Christ is The Hope of Men!

John Gowans

Stories of light and darkness can be found in abundance. They play out all around us. If we are paying attention, we will see them, regardless of the quality of visibility on any given day. Here's one I found recently. I think it at least begins to get at what Gowans was communicating in his light song:

"I hope so, 'cause it's coming either way," Jesse used to

say when her mother asked if she was ready for the next day. Then they would share a little laugh. Tucking her tightly into her warm bed and switching on the bedside nightlight, Jesse's mother would sing her daughter a simple song which her mother had sung to her:

Hope, like the sunrise, chases the shadows.
Darkness resists in vain.
Nothing can crush it. Nothing can kill it.
Buried it lives again!
Buried it lives again!
Sleep now, to wake again.

But that was before the thunder, lightning and flood had taken away Jesse's parents, along with her home and any hope she ever had of being ready for the next day. Laughter, light and sweet songs now seemed a world away from her. They had been replaced by tears, darkness and menacing messages.

"Thunder and lightning, very, very frightening! Boom, boom, out go the lights!" were the last, chilling words Jesse had heard every night for the past six years. They were spoken in a kind of hideous hush by Judge E. Bryl, head keeper, just before he switched the dorm lights off and closed the locked door, leaving the girl in the dark, alone. Ever since a police officer found her sleeping on the wet pavement outside an old abandoned church and brought her to the dilapidated and dreary Home for the Hopeless, Jesse had gone to sleep each night trying her hardest to subdue the fear those words created within her. Now, on the eve of her 18th birthday, with tomorrow's Mandatory Exit looming large, she wondered if this would be the last night she would be required to hear those words, or if they would echo in her ears, haunting her throughout her lifetime. She wouldn't have to wait long to find out.

What seemed like a few short hours later, Jesse woke to the sound of children laughing. It was early. Or was it late? Either way, Judge Bryl and his staff would not rise for at least another few hours. As she walked to the window, the sound of the laughter grew louder, and she couldn't hold back a curious giggle of her own. Laughter was a luxury she rarely allowed herself. Not that there was ever much reason to indulge. But certainly one could be forgiven for laughter lapses on one's birthday. As she pulled back the burlap curtain, an invasion of light flooded her room, leaving no previously darkened corner untransformed. When her eyes adjusted to the brightness, she looked out her window to the lawn below. There she saw the source of the laughter. Three children were pretending to do battle. Brandishing Styrofoam swords and holding tightly to cardboard shields, they ran after invisible enemies. With the enthusiasm of a child heading toward a surprise on her birthday, she hurried into her robe, skipped down the stairs and darted outside. But the commotion must've woken Judge Bryl, because he arrived at the scene of the battle mere seconds after Jesse. In his pinstriped nightgown, complete with "J.E.B." monogrammed in black and red thread, he might have looked funny, if the look on his face wasn't so frightening.

Upon the arrival of the young girl and her warden, the attention of the three visitors was drawn away from their invisible war, and the laughter immediately ceased. It was only then that Jesse noticed that the light which had engulfed her room moments before emanated from the Styrofoam swords and cardboard shields. The rest of the surroundings—the yard, the home, the gravel road—were still swallowed up by the darkness of the deepest night.

"I demand to know the meaning of this?" screamed Bryl.

"And that's precisely why you most likely never will," replied one of the young warriors, while thrusting her sword into the head keeper's shin.

Bryl was less affected by the play sword than by the sting of the verbal rebuke. "Who are you and what are you doing on private property?"

"This property may be private, but it isn't hidden. And what has been done here has not been done in secret," spoke another of the children, in a voice well beyond the years his height and appearance suggested.

"I should hope not," replied Bryl. "I have provided food and shelter to lost children for years, at no small personal expense I might add."

"Your food is fear, and it has been force fed to innocents. Your shelter is a drapery of darkness, designed to frighten little ones nearly to death," boomed the third of the freedom fighters.

This third word of hard truth was followed immediately by a chorus, sung in unison by the three playful combatants:

> Candle, lantern, sunrise
> Darkness, shadows, fear
> Three will last forever
> Three will die right here

> Candle, Lantern, Sunrise
> He who lights the way
> Sent us here for Jesse
> You will have to stay.

As a benediction of sorts, one of the three stared directly into Bryl's eyes, smiled, and added, "Boom, boom, out go the lights!" For the second time in a very long time, Jesse let a laugh escape her lips. And with that, the three beings scooped Jesse up in their little, strong arms and vanished in a flash of lightning and to the crash of thunder. The judge was left standing alone in the darkness, scratching his head and rubbing his shin.

When Jesse was safe and sound in her new home, she inquired from the three little liberators as to what kind of life she could expect, now that she was on her own. "On your own?" they replied in shocked unison. "You've never been on your own in the past, and you never will be in the future." Seeing the unanswered questions in her eyes, they spent several hours giving Jesse some pointers, including a Styrofoam sword of her own. Before they left, they asked Jesse if she was ready for tomorrow. "Yes," she stated with some certainty.

> Lord be my light and be my salvation
> All I want is to be in the light of love
> All I want is to be in the light.
> —Charlie Peacock

A Motley Crew

You let some funny people
Work for You,
And Your disciples are
A motley crew!
The limited
The damaged
And the lame
Do daily wonders
In Your holy Name.

They're far from perfect;
You don't seem to mind.
They're far from worthy
And You're far too kind!

You still prefer,
I note with glad surprise,
To use the weak things
To confound the wise!

John Gowans

Have you ever stopped to wonder why God chose to use some of the flawed men and women we meet in the Bible? If you have, you've probably already come to the realization that it wasn't as though there were only a handful of them that had issues—most of them did. This fact can either concern or comfort us. It's easy to see why some Christians would rather ignore, downplay or explain away the shortcomings of their favorite Bible character. We need our heroes to be super. We prefer saints of the spotless variety. So, we often conveniently skip over the more earthy aspects of their character and the bumpier parts of their journeys. As I write this, Darren Aronofsky's modern epic *Noah* is the talk of the town hall. While the film is playing at multiplexes all over the country, conversations about some of the more controversial filmmaking choices are playing out all over social media. It's difficult to log onto Facebook without half of your Christian friends telling you to go see it and the other half questioning your salvation if you do see it. Meanwhile, your other friends are most likely avoiding the whole mess in favor of seeing *Frozen* for the 10th time. Not wanting to offend my readership, I am leery of tipping my hand here as to my personal views of the film *Noah*. Having said that, I thought it was awesome! One of the main issues the film's Christian critics have is that Noah isn't saintly enough. They're right. He wasn't. And God still chose to use Noah. And Noah still chose to obey God.

Certainly there are thematic elements of *Noah* that aren't suitable for small children. But that goes for the film as well as the Biblical account. And speaking of the children, it just wouldn't do to have the kids in our churches learn the whole, sordid truth. Think about it, have you ever heard a Sunday school chorus focusing on Abram/Abraham twice passing his wife Sarai/Sarah off as his sister, in order to save his own skin? I don't think so. If you have, please send it to me. I'd like to hear it. The prevailing rule when it comes to Biblical bios seems to have taken its cue from a 1944 Johnny Mercer sermon-song:

> You've got to accentuate the positive
> Eliminate the negative

Latch on to the affirmative
But don't mess with Mister In-Between.

This practice seems harmless, right? I mean, why do the kiddies need to know the shameful shenanigans "only a little boy, David" got into years after "the giant came tumbling down"? Well, maybe they don't need to be dished all the dirt at a young age. All in good time, right? But to never acknowledge the sinfulness of Scripture's main characters is problematic for (at least) three reasons:

1. The good, bad and ugly stuff is right there in black and white. To exclude something God has included seems dangerous at best (and disastrous at worst).

2. If we skip the appalling parts, we may not catch the full force of the amazing parts.

3. If we read, teach and sing only sanitized Scripture lessons, we run the risk of buying into the lies that our lives should be trouble-free, and that God only uses perfect people. This third problem is two-pronged: setting the bar too high to reach—thus stressing us out—and discouraging and disqualifying us from the hope that God would choose us for something miraculous (setting his people free, feeding 5,000 plus people, healing the hurts of OTHERS).

Here's good news: God still chooses and uses fallen and flawed individuals.

An author who has made a huge impact on me is Brennan Manning. He is now perfected, as he went to be with his Abba on April 12, 2013 (almost a year to the day from this writing). In the first chapter of his great work, *The Ragamuffin Gospel: Good News for the Bedraggled, Beat-Up, and Burnt Out*, he encourages us to take an honest look at ourselves, and not let that look keep us from seeing God and all he has for us:

> When I get honest, I admit I am a bundle of paradoxes. I believe and I doubt, I hope and get discouraged, I love and I hate, I feel bad about feeling good, I feel guilty about not feeling guilty. I am trusting and suspicious. I am honest and I still play games. Aristotle said I am a rational animal; I say I am an angel with an incredible capacity for beer. To live by grace means to acknowledge my whole life story, the light side and the dark. In admitting my shadow side I learn who I am and what God's grace means. As Thomas Merton put it, "A saint is not someone who is good but who experiences the goodness of God."

I think this is what John Gowans was getting at in the poem we consider here. In his 1981 *O Lord!* book of poems, this piece is titled *Oddities*. Gowans takes comfort ("with glad surprise") in the fact that God used and continues to use people that we might not deem worthy. Why? My guess is that he knew himself well enough to know that he was "far from perfect … far from worthy." I join him (Don't you?) in glad surprise that God uses "the limited, the damaged and the lame," and that he still chooses *the foolish things of the world to shame the wise … the weak things of the world to shame the strong* (1 Cor. 1:27).

Dream On

Must there be always suffering, always pain?
Must hatred always rule, love never reign?
Must there be discord and dissent?
Must there be tears and discontent?

I dream of a day
Not far, far away
When in the world of men, the love of God shall be seen
All tears shall be dried
All needs satisfied
Where men are warring now, the peace of God intervene
This dream comes true wherever Christ is crowned
His coming stills the storm of strife
Wherever Jesus reigns, there joy is found
And hope and peace and love and light

Can flowers flourish where the thorns have grown?
Can care, at last, be forced to leave her throne?
Can blinded men be made to see?
Can truth imprisoned, be set free?

John Gowans

John Gowans was born in 1934 in Blantyre, South La-narkshire, Scotland. Six years later, John Lennon was born in Liverpool, England, a little over three hours by car from Gowans' birthplace. Interestingly, they died on the same day,

December 8. Lennon, of course, was killed in 1980 by an assassin's bullet. Gowans died in 2012, after a long period of declining health. In addition to being born six years apart in the same part of the world and dying on the same day 32 years apart, the two Johns also shared a way with words and were both dreamers.

Lennon's dream is forever immortalized in his 1971 song, "Imagine." In the song, Lennon imagines a world where there is no heaven, no hell, no countries, no religion, no possessions and no need for greed or hunger. In this dream, "all the people" live for today, in peace, "sharing all the world." Later in the song, Lennon imagines that many will dismiss his vision of unity and write him off as a dreamer. But the songwriter turns the insult into an invitation:

> You may say I'm a dreamer
> But I'm not the only one
> I hope someday you'll join us
> And the world will be as one.

You may or may not share Lennon's imagination. You may or may not accept his invitation to join him. But you'd be hard pressed to question his credentials as a dreamer. I mean, world unity? That is not a dwarfed dream. That's big time! It may not fit nicely into your theology, but at some level you've got to appreciate the audacity of it all, don't you?

John Gowans was a dreamer as well. In 1967, at about the same time Lennon and the other Fab Three released their seminal *Sgt. Pepper's* album, Gowans' song, "I Dream of a Day," saw the light of day. While he doesn't quite outline a vision of world unity in the song, he does express hopes for giving peace a chance. The first verse is a psalm of lament, with Gowans asking how long humankind will have to contend with suffering, pain, hatred, discord, dissent, tears and discontent. Then the dream transports the author and, one would hope, his audience to a place where love reigns supreme. A place where all tears are dried and all needs are satisfied; a place where the love of God is seen and the peace of God intervenes. But this isn't some pipe dream for Gowans. He's not even dreaming of a day when he will walk on streets of gold and live in a mansion. Gowans is not dreaming of a day far, far away. No way! This dream of his comes true "wherever Christ is crowned ... wherever Jesus reigns."

In the seventh chapter of Luke's gospel, we find some disciples of John the Baptist asking Jesus if he is the one they had been expecting:

> *In the next two or three hours Jesus healed many from diseases, distress, and evil spirits. To many of the blind he gave the gift of sight. Then he gave his answer: "Go back and tell John what you have just seen and heard: The blind see, the lame walk, lepers are cleansed, the deaf hear, the dead are raised, the wretched of the earth have God's salvation hospitality extended to them. Is this what you were expecting? Then count yourselves fortunate!"* (vv. 21-23 MSG).

Is this what you imagined? Is this the day you've been dreaming of?

In their dreams, both Lennon and Gowans acknowledge that there is certainly enough to keep us up at night. And yet they dared to dream. What about you? What about me? Are we content with a good night's sleep, or will we allow the cares of a fallen creation to give us some fitful nights, resulting in some faith-full dreams?

Giant Power

At the moment of my weakness, when my need for power is plain,
And my own strength is exhausted once again,
Then my Lord has made provision for the day of my despair,
And his precious Holy Spirit hears my prayer, my prayer
Then my Lord has made provision for the day of my despair,
And his precious Holy Spirit hears my prayer.

Holy Spirit! Promised Presence, fall on me.
Holy Spirit! Make me all I long to be.
Holy Spirit! Holy Spirit!
Give your power to me, O Holy Spirit.

When the darkness falls around me, when bewildered and afraid,
When I feel the most deserted and betrayed,
Then my every need is answered by God's providential care,
And his precious Holy Spirit hears my prayer, my prayer,
Then my every need is answered by God's providential care,
And his precious Holy Spirit hears my prayer.

Nothing now can rob God's servant of the peace that he bequeaths,
Nothing take away the strength his presence breathes.
Of the everlasting arms of love I'm daily made aware,
And his precious Holy Spirit hears my prayer, my prayer.
Of the everlasting arms of love I'm daily made aware,
And his precious Holy Spirit hears my prayer.

John Gowans

"But you will receive power when the Holy Spirit comes on you" (Acts 1:8).

We've all had moments of weakness, when our "strength is exhausted" and our "need for power is plain." If you haven't, check your pulse—quick! In the opening lyric of this stunning song, Gowans touches on a core component of the human condition. We all know the feeling of helplessness that can come on in an instant, paralyzing us. Our body readies for either fight or flight, but neither comes easily. To turn a phrase, the flesh is willing, but the spirit is weak. In those situations, even seemingly little obstacles seem huge, casting giant shadows over any sense of peace we might usually know, zapping us of any power we might usually own.

Speaking of giant shadows, Fezzik casts one in the 1987 film *The Princess Bride*. He is one of three outlaws who kidnap Buttercup in the hopes of starting a war for her fiancé, Prince Humperdink. But The Man in Black (Westley, Buttercup's true love) is in hot pursuit of the outlaws. He is intent on rescuing his love. After scaling the über-dangerous Cliffs of Insanity and winning an amazing sword fight with Inigo Montoya, Westley encounters Fezzik, a wall of a man played by former WWF Champion wrestler André the Giant. Fezzik challenges Westley to a hand-to-hand fight to the finish ("as God intended").

Westley: I think the odds are slightly in your favor at hand fighting.

Fezzik: It's not my fault—being the biggest and the strongest. I don't even exercise.

Later in the fight, when Westley's strength is exhausted

29

and his need for power is plain, he questions Fezzik, "Look, are you just fiddling around with me or what?" to which the gentle giant replies, "I just want you to feel you are doing well. I hate for people to die embarrassed." Finally, after a few minutes of hanging on the giant's back and wearing him out, Westley defeats Fezzik with a strangle-hold. He doesn't kill him, however. In fact, before he leaves to share iocaine powder-laced drinks with Vizzini, the "mastermind" of the kidnapping, Westley advises Fezzik to "rest well and dream of large women."

Giant fights aren't confined to the summit of the Cliffs of Insanity. One took place in the Valley of Elah. King Saul and his Israelite forces were preparing to do battle with the Philistine army. 1 Samuel 17:3-10 (MSG) sets the stage this way:

> The Philistines were on one hill, the Israelites on the opposing hill, with the valley between them.
>
> A giant nearly ten feet tall stepped out from the Philistine line into the open, Goliath from Gath. He had a bronze helmet on his head and was dressed in armor—126 pounds of it! He wore bronze shin guards and carried a bronze sword. His spear was like a fence rail—the spear tip alone weighed over fifteen pounds. His shield bearer walked ahead of him.
>
> Goliath stood there and called out to the Israelite troops, "Why bother using your whole army? Am I not Philistine enough for you? And you're all committed to Saul, aren't you? So pick your best fighter and pit him against me. If he gets the upper hand and kills me, the Philistines will all become your slaves. But if I get the upper hand and kill him, you'll all become our slaves and serve us. I challenge the troops of Israel this day. Give me a man. Let us fight it out together!"

Clearly, Goliath was no friendly Fezzik. This man was out for blood. He wanted to kill someone! Verse 16 tells us that Goliath taunted this taunt every morning and every evening for 40 days, terrifying the Israelites and causing them to lose all hope (v. 11). The men of Israel were not manning up. David was the youngest of eight sons of Jesse. His three oldest brothers had followed Saul to war. At the request of his father, David brought food to his brothers at the front lines. While there, he heard the giant's threats and couldn't understand why they went unchallenged by the army of the living God. When he was called to the king, this conversation transpired:

> "Master," said David, "don't give up hope. I'm ready to go and fight this Philistine."
>
> Saul answered David, "You can't go and fight this Philistine. You're too young and inexperienced—and he's been at this fighting business since before you were born."
>
> David said, "I've been a shepherd, tending sheep for my father. Whenever a lion or bear came and took a lamb from the flock, I'd go after it, knock it down, and rescue the lamb. If it turned on me, I'd grab it by the throat, wring its neck, and kill it. Lion or bear, it made no difference—I killed it. And I'll do the same to this Philistine pig who is taunting the troops of God-Alive. God, who delivered me from the teeth of the lion and the claws of the bear, will deliver me from this Philistine."
>
> Saul said, "Go. And God help you!" (1 Sam. 17:32-37 MSG).

You know the rest of this fight to the finish better than I would be able to tell it. Suffice it to say, there is truth to the adage, "The bigger they are, the harder they fall." David may have played a harp, but he was also into hard rock (and that day, hard rock was into Goliath). But it wasn't simply a sling and a stone that slew the giant in the Valley of Elah. The Spirit was the secret weapon. Here's the way it works. Before 1 Samuel 17, there was 1 Samuel 16. Before Goliath called David out to kill him, the Lord had called David out to crown him. Before the power came, the presence came. Before the stoning of Goliath, there was the Spirit on David: *So Samuel took the horn of oil and anointed him in the presence of his brothers, and from that day on the Spirit of the Lord came powerfully upon David* (1 Sam. 16:13).

In the introduction for his 2013 book, *David and Goliath: Underdogs, Misfits, and the Art of Battling Giants*, author Malcolm Gladwell writes, "David and Goliath is a book about what happens when ordinary people confront giants. By 'giants,' I mean powerful opponents of all kinds—from armies and mighty warriors to disability, misfortune and oppression."

So, how do the giant battles of fictional Westley and Biblical David inform and inspire our own? It seems to me that when we wonder if the giants we face are just fiddling around with us, making us feel we are doing well before we die, there is still hope. When we hear them spewing taunts, we can respond with Spirit-filled truths. When we feel that we don't have a prayer, we do. There is a promise. There is a presence. And there *is* power.

PRAYER
All-powerful God, give me power (and a good aim). Amen.

All Apologetic

Kneeling in penitence I make my prayer,
Owning my weaknesses and my despair;
Failure I cannot hide,
Broken my selfish pride,
Pardon thou dost provide,
Pardon declare.

Nothing can I achieve, nothing attain;
He that without thee builds, labors in vain;
Shatter my own design,
Shaping a plan divine,
Come to this heart of mine,
Saviour, again.

Though few the gifts I have that thou canst use,
Make thy demands on me; I'll not refuse;
Take all there is of me,
Take what I hope to be;
Thy way at last I see,
Thy way I choose.

John Gowans

Wikipedia (yes, I went there, get over it) defines apologetics as "the discipline of defending a position (often religious) through the systematic use of information." Christian apologists have been around since there was a Christian position to defend. The apostle Paul was, arguably, the first in a long line of disciplined defenders such as Augustine of Hippo, Thomas Aquinas, Blaise Pascal, G.K. Chesterton, C.S. Lewis, Ravi Zacharias and Lee Strobel. In different centuries, in different languages and in different ways, Christian apologists have endeavored to reason with people, in the hopes of convincing them and converting them. But rational thought does not guarantee radical transformation. As R.C. Sproul wrote in a *Tabletalk* article in July 1991, "No amount of rational argument, cogent evidence, or forceful persuasion can change the heart of the unbeliever unless that sinner is first regenerated by God the Holy Spirit .... I am in total agreement with the thesis that apologetics alone cannot convert the sinner. But I do not further conclude that apologetics is therefore unnecessary." In the article, Sproul offers four "vital tasks" of apologetics—pre-evangelism, restraining evil, supporting believers and intellectual credibility—in order to help shape culture.

It's not my job to diss the discipline of apologetics. In fact, I wouldn't do it even if it was my job. What a weird job that would be! The truth is I have the utmost respect for anyone who can speak clearly and courageously for the cause of Christ. And if they can do so courteously, that's a bonus. There's a guy here in San Francisco who could use some training in that last department. He seems to have answered the call to "judgment evangelism," and from my 6th floor office I can often hear him yelling into his bullhorn at passersby. I'm not sure "Bullhorn Guy" (thanks, Rob Bell and NOOMA) would call himself an apologist, but what he's doing definitely calls for an apology. Or maybe how I view and judge him calls for an apology on my part? Which reminds me, that is what I really wanted to write about—an apology.

Hopefully you can forgive me the mistake. After all, "apologetics" and "apology" are related to the same Greek word "apologia." And back in the day, as I've already mentioned, to make an apology did mean to offer a statement in defense of a position. It can still be used in that context of course, but in everyday speak, offering an apology means admitting wrongdoing and regretting having done it. Most often, when we say people are apologetic we mean they have confessed that they can offer no defense of their position.

That is exactly the position in which we find the main character of this Gowans song, "kneeling in penitence," realizing that he or she has failed, perhaps failed again and again. This penitent offers no defense, just prayers for pardon. That's a safe, sweet place to be. It's not dissimilar to the place the prophet Isaiah found himself as he was caught up in a vision of the glory of God, as recorded in the sixth chapter of Isaiah. He is confronted by God's holiness (vv. 1-4), convicted of and cleansed of his own sinfulness (vv. 5-7), and he is commissioned to a life of usefulness (vv. 8-13). The three verses of this song describe the same penitent progression: praying for pardon, seeking the Savior, devoting to discipleship.

Not all of us are gifted in the discipline of apologetics. All of us owe an apology. And the good news for us is the same good news that awaited Isaiah, and it is the same good news found in this song; pardon is provided.

If we confess our sins, he is faithful and just and will
forgive us our sins and purify us from all unrighteousness
(1 John 1:9).

NOTE: For an insightful teaching on Isaiah 6, I recommend a dated, but dynamic, message from R.C. Sproul (apologist) called "The Importance of Holiness." Go ahead, Google it and watch it. If you don't like it … well, my apologies.

Burning, Burning

Burning, burning, brightly burning,
Brightly burning Fire divine,
Satisfy my spirit's yearning.
Fill this empty soul of mine.

Burning, burning, always burning.
Holy Spirit, stay with me;
To your will my will is turning,
What you will I want to be.

Burning, burning, deeply burning,
Deeply burning holy Fire,
Now, your perfect plan discerning,
Your design is my desire.

Burning, burning, gently burning,
Gently burning Fire within,
From your love my love is learning.
Now I feel your work begin.

John Gowans

I currently work in San Francisco, California. It's a great, international city, full of life. The city has been the subject of songs from singers as diverse as Tony Bennett and Brett Dennen. In a 1967 song sung by Scott McKenzie, we're offered this helpful piece of advice: "If you're going to San Francisco, be sure to wear some flowers in your hair." Groups such as Journey and Train have sung unabashedly about their love for this iconic town. And speaking of groups, on August 29, 1966, a little band from Liverpool, England, played their last live concert at San Francisco's Candlestick Park, former home of the two-time (or seven-time, depending on how you count it) World Series champion Giants, and not far from my own home (which I don't own).

As if that wasn't enough to prove this city's awesomeness, millions of kids all over the U.S.—and anywhere fine American television programming is exported—have grown up knowing San Francisco as the hometown of Danny, Joey, Uncle Jesse, D.J., Stephanie, cute little Michelle (both of them) and the rest of the "Full House" gang. I don't want to brag, but one of the first things our family did when we moved here in 2009 was to drive to Lower Pacific Heights and take pictures at the house and nearby Alamo Square Park depicted in the show's opening credits. Jealous much? Hopefully not. Anyway, in a "Full House" episode titled "Aftershocks," which aired a few months after San Francisco's 1989 Loma Prieta earthquake, Danny (Dad) has to figure out how to deal with how Stephanie (middle daughter) is dealing with the quake. **SPOILER ALERT**: Everything works out alright.

On April 19, 1906, 83 years before that fictional and factual quake, *The Call-Chronicle-Examiner's* headline read, "EARTHQUAKE AND FIRE: SAN FRANCISCO IN RUINS." The reports told the terrifying stories of the great city of San Francisco being shaken up and burned down. Misery, pain and need were everywhere. Diseases, including tuberculosis, diphtheria, small pox, measles and scarlet fever, were on the rise. It is difficult to overstate the devastation that San Francisco suffered that day. A quake lasting only 46 seconds all but leveled a major North American city, killing more than 3,000 people and leaving over 200,000 people without homes. Fires lasting three days and nights were more devastating than the quake itself.

From childhood, we are warned of the dangers of fire. "Don't play with matches" has most likely been in the lexicon for parents ever since matches were invented. Before that, parents used to tell their kids not to rub two sticks together quickly while blowing in that direction. (I may have made up that last "fact.") Anyway, it doesn't take a huge natural disaster to convince us of fire's destructive power. But there are other ways in which firepower is experienced. In Genesis, chapter 22, Abraham carried fire and a knife to demonstrate the power of obedience. In the third chapter of Exodus, Yahweh appeared to Moses in flames of fire within a bush, while 10 chapters later the power of his presence and protection was evidenced to the children of Israel by a pillar of fire each night. In Exodus, chapter 19, Moses returns to the foot of Mount Sinai, as commanded, to find it *covered with smoke, because the Lord descended on it in fire* (v. 18). To the prophet Jeremiah, God's Word was in his heart like a fire, one so powerfully hot, it could not be contained (Jer. 20:9). The Old Testament references to the power of fire are too numerous to list here, so let's skip ahead to a few New Testament flames.

> *"I baptize you with water. But one who is more powerful than I will come, the straps of whose sandals I am not worthy to untie. He will baptize you with the Holy Spirit and fire"* (Luke 3:16, spoken by John the Baptist).

> *Suddenly a sound like the blowing of a violent wind came from heaven and filled the whole house where they were sitting. They saw what seemed to be tongues of fire that separated and came to rest on each of them. All of them were filled with the Holy Spirit and began to speak in other tongues as the Spirit enabled them* (Acts 2:2-4).

The Fire John prophesied about at the Jordan River was the Fire present in that Jerusalem room. It is that same Fire that John Gowans writes about in these three verses and a chorus. It is the "brightly," "deeply," "gently burning" Fire of the Holy Spirit. It is this Fire—and only this Fire—that satisfies our "spirit's yearning," and fills our "empty soul." This "Fire divine," this "holy Fire," is the "Fire within" the lives of all who have trusted Jesus to save them. This Fire cannot be contained or quenched. This Fire doesn't go out after three days and nights. This Fire is "always burning." This Fire builds instead of destroys (except in the case of evil strongholds). This Fire brings healing, not disease. This Fire offers life, not death.

As I mentioned in this volume's introduction, John Gowans served as the international leader of The Salvation Army for a little over three years, from July 1999 to September 2002. One of the mottos of our movement, taking center stage in our flag, is "blood and fire." We want the world to know that the blood of Jesus—shed for humankind's sin—cleanses, and the fire of the Holy Spirit—in the life of every believer—has the firepower to keep that believer clean. This is one Fire that we want to spread, uncontrollably. The heat is on. Can you feel it?

Counting Crows

(and Prayers and Naps and Denials and Fish
and Resurrection Appearances and "I Love You"s)

Knowing my failings, knowing my fears,
Seeing my sorrow, drying my tears.
Jesus recall me, me re-ordain;
You know I love you, use me again.

I have no secrets unknown to you,
No special graces, talents are few;
Yet your intention I would fulfill;
You know I love you, ask what you will.

For the far future I cannot see,
Promise your presence, travel with me;
Sunshine or shadows? I cannot tell;
You know I love you, all will be well.

John Gowans

It's a common misconception that the rooster in the passion narrative crowed three times, once for each of Peter's denials. It *may* have crowed three times, of course. Roosters are free to crow as often as they like. The point is Jesus didn't say the rooster would crow three times and the Bible doesn't record that the rooster crowed three times. Let's set the record straight right here. In Matthew 26:34, Luke 22:34 and John 13:38, Jesus prophesizes Peter's three denials, and says they will occur before the crow of the rooster. In Mark 14:30, the three denials are prophesied to take place before two crows from the rooster. In Mark 14:72, after Peter vehemently denied even knowing Jesus, the rooster crowed a second time.

There you have it—three denials, but only one (or two) rooster crows. I'm not sure why people think the rooster crowed three times. Maybe it's because there were three denials, so we automatically attribute a crow for each. Maybe it's that the words twice and thrice are so similar. Maybe the story is so familiar to us that we don't know it all that well. If that is the reason, something's wrong. We should know Peter's story—intimately. Why? I think it's because Peter's story of failings and fears and sorrow and tears is our story of failings and fears and sorrow and tears. That is, of course, unless you have never failed Jesus. If that is the case, put down this book and go straight to heaven. The rest of us can relate to Peter's ability to fail his friend three times before the rooster could even get a crow (or two crows) out. If we're honest, we see ourselves in Peter's denials. We should be able to empathize with him, having denied knowing Jesus at some point (or many points) in our own lives. Hey, it's no big deal if we make little mistakes while counting crows. But it is a HUGE deal if we miss out on identifying with Jesus Christ.

In Philippians 3:10-11, the apostle Paul expressed his deep desire to identify with Jesus: *I want to know Christ— yes, to know the power of his resurrection and participation in his sufferings, becoming like him in his death, and so, somehow, attaining to the resurrection from the dead.* Maybe if Peter could have read these verses, he would have been inspired to throw his lot in with his Lord. That would've been impossible, of course, because they hadn't yet been written at the time when the rooster was crowin' and Peter was denyin'. But Peter had no excuse. He had spent three of the best years of his life with Jesus. Jesus had convinced him and his brother Andrew to give up fishing for fish and take up fishing for people. Jesus had healed his mother-in-law (Careful guys!). Jesus had called Peter out to walk on water with him (then saved him from drowning). Jesus had even changed Peter's name from Simon to, well, Peter. And just before Jesus predicted Peter's three denials (and the rooster's one or two crows), he washed Peter's feet. In response to talk of betrayals that night, Peter declared, *"Even if I have to die with you, I will never disown you"* (Matt. 26:35).

Garden.
    Jesus.
        Praying.
            Thrice.
                Peter.
                    Sleeping.
                        Thrice.
                            Betrayer.
                            Swords.
                                Clubs.
                                  Kiss.
                                    Arrest.
                                      Desertion.
                                      Courtyard.
                                          Denial.
                                          Denial.
                                            Denial.

The Alarm, an 80s band I used to (read: still do) listen to, have a song called "Where Were You Hiding When the Storm Broke?" Included in the lyrics is this great line, "They say that all things come in threes, well here comes the third degree." So far in Peter's story, even though the rooster only crowed once or twice, there have been a few things (prayers, naps, denials) that have come in threes.

Well, here comes the third degree.

In the 21st chapter of John's gospel, we find Peter and six other disciples fishing (for fish) unsuccessfully all night. From the shore, Jesus called to them, instructing them to cast their nets on the *right* side of the boat. Soon it became obvious that they had been casting their nets on the *wrong* side of the boat before listening to Jesus (Can you relate?), as they couldn't even bring in all the fish they caught. Then John said to Peter, "*It is the Lord*" (v. 7). When Peter heard this, he jumped into the water. Apparently his surface-skipping days were history, but we can assume he kept his eyes focused on Jesus this time, nevertheless. Jesus told his followers to bring the fish they had just caught. Peter, anxious to please the Master he had denied, hauled to shore the 153 (divisible by three, btw) fresh fish. John makes a point of telling us in verse 14 that this was the third post-resurrection appearance Jesus had made to his disciples.

After sharing breakfast together, Jesus asked Peter the same question three times, "*Do you love me*?" Peter offered the same reply three times, "*You know that I love you*" (the same words in the last line of each of the three verses in this Gowans piece). Jesus' three replies to Peter's three replies were almost identical: "*Feed my lambs; Take care of my sheep; Feed my sheep*" (vv. 15-17). Beautiful, right? After Peter denied Jesus three times, he was given three opportunities to proclaim his love for his Lord. And to top it all off, Jesus gave him a mission. Earlier I suggested to you that Peter's story is our story. At the time, that might not have seemed like such great news. After all, we were relating to his "failings," "fears," "sorrows" and "tears," as Gowans puts it. Now, however, those of us who are honest with ourselves would admit that we desperately need Peter's story to be our own. We can't deny similar denials of Jesus, but we hope for similar healing from Jesus and we ache for similar acceptance from Jesus.

PRAYER

Jesus, I deeply regret denying you. You know I love you. I love you. I love you. Use me again. Ask what you will. All will be well. Amen.

Concerned for the City?

Do you love cities,
Crowded squares and shops;
The clanging street car;
Coffee-bars and cops;
The concrete sidewalk
And the grey sky-scraper;
The garish night-signs
And the gusts of paper?

It seems unlikely
But perhaps You do,
And wish the cities would
Make room for You.
There's so much sadness
And it's such a pity.
I understand You wept once
For a city?

John Gowans

I am contemplating and writing about this Gowans poem on a Saturday, Lazarus Saturday to be exact. Never heard of it? If not, that would make me feel much better, because I had not heard of it until today. Or, if I had, I cannot remember ever hearing of it. Lazarus Saturday is the day before Palm Sunday and, in the Eastern Orthodox Church, commemorates the raising of the grateful, formerly dead Lazarus to life by his good friend, Jesus (John 11:1-44). That passage of Scripture contains the favorite Sunday school memory verse of all time, *Jesus wept* (v. 35). Some contend the tears came as a result of the lack of faith expressed by Mary, Martha and the mourners. Others argue that he cried because his friend had died. Maybe he cried because he knew that over 2,000 years later, his followers would be more concerned with such arguments than the fact that the dead can be raised. Whatever the reason, Jesus wept.

Tomorrow (it follows, after Lazarus Saturday) is Palm Sunday, commemorating Jesus' final entry into Jerusalem. The way Luke tells it in chapter 19 of his gospel account, Jesus rode on a donkey into the city. As he entered, people spread their cloaks on the road (v. 36). By the way, why did "Cloak Sunday" never catch on? As he approached Jerusalem and saw the city, Luke writes, *he wept over it* (v. 41). Why did Jesus weep this time? After all, his friend Lazarus was alive, thanks to the resurrection power of God. Luke is clear that tears came to the eyes of Jesus when he saw the city. Why?

Was it smoggy like L.A.? Was it rainy like Seattle? Was it windy like Chicago? Was it foggy like London or San Francisco? Was it stinky like _____? (Fill in the name of your least favorite Smellville.)

As is often the case, we need only to look at Scripture to find the answer. In verses 42-44 of chapter 19, Luke records the reason for the tears. Jesus knew what could bring peace to Jerusalem, and what would bring destruction to that city. His tears were an expression of mourning, this time not for a dead friend, but for a dying city—a city whose enemies would destroy it, a city whose inhabitants would be dashed to the ground. A city that "*did not recognize the time of God's coming*" to them (v. 44). By this point, Jesus knew what would happen to him in Jerusalem. He was not crying for his own death, but for the deaths of those he loved in that great city.

We are called to be Christlike. Sometimes that pursuit will bring tears to our eyes for lack of faith (our own, or someone else's). Sometimes that pursuit will bring tears to our eyes over a friend's passing. At other times, however, tears should flood our eyes due to the realization that the very people Jesus died to save are dying. I intentionally chose the word "should" in the last sentence because the sad, tear-worthy fact is that the tears don't always come to us, even with the realization that countless citizens of great cities are headed for destruction when peace could be theirs. It's not a stretch to think that tears may still be coming to the eyes of Jesus if we aren't helping people recognize the time of God's coming to them.

In 1987, I attended InterVarsity's Urbana Student Missions Conference. The theme that year was, "Should I Not Be Concerned?" and was taken from the 4th chapter of Jonah. After Jonah had run away from the call of God to preach to Nineveh; after he had been thrown overboard from his getaway boat; after he had been swallowed (and saved) by a huge fish; after he had preached and prophesied on the streets of Nineveh; after God had relented and held back the destruction of that city and its citizens; after God had given and taken away a plant to shade Jonah's hot head, we find Jonah with a bad attitude and a death wish (Jonah 4:1-3, 8-9). He is angry that his plant was taken away, sure, but he is most likely still angry that God proved himself to be a *"gracious and compassionate God, slow to anger and abounding in love, a God who relents from sending calamity"* (Jonah 4:2). God's reply is classic, and I have heard his voice speak various versions of this to me during periods of my life when I've had too much whine: *"You have been concerned about this plant, though you did not tend it or make it grow. It sprang up overnight and died overnight. And should I not have concern for the great city of Nineveh, in which there are more than a hundred and twenty thousand people who cannot tell their right hand from their left—and also many animals?"* (Jonah 4:10-11). Should I not have concern for the great city?

There were many great speakers at Urbana in 1987, including Billy Graham, Tony Compolo, Rebecca Pippert, and Ray Bakke. One morning, Floyd McClung of Youth With A Mission (YWAM) spoke about the work of the gospel in Amsterdam. By 1987, his family had lived there for 14 years. They lived in the red light district, which was 12 blocks long and six blocks wide, with 16,000 prostitutes and 12,000 drug addicts. When he first arrived in Amsterdam, he would walk around trying to get a feel for God's heartbeat for the city. It seems to me that's what Jonah didn't do for Nineveh, but what Jesus did do for Jerusalem on Palm (or Cloak) Sunday. It is what I have done for some cities, for some people, but not for others. It is what we are all called to do—follow the heartbeat of God into the city. Heartbeat. Tears. Sacrifice. Lazarus Saturdays. Palm Sundays. Good Fridays. Easter Sundays. Thanks to Jesus, we get to experience all of it. We get to help OTHERS recognize the time of God's coming to them.

During his talk at Urbana 87, Floyd McClung spoke of the impact of the Billy Graham International Congress for Itinerate Evangelists, which had convened in Amsterdam the year before. "Can you imagine 10,000 evangelists sitting in a conference for two weeks without preaching? It was impossible … every tram and train and bus had moving street meetings. My wife was walking down a street one day and she heard a man mumbling to himself … 'Oh, Jesus, Jesus, Jesus,' then she heard the man add, 'Everywhere I go I get nothing but Jesus.'"

May it be so in your city and mine. Amen

Sweet, Sweet Song of Discipleship

If crosses come, if it should cost me dearly
To be the servant of my Servant Lord;
If darkness falls around the path of duty,
And men despise the Saviour I've adored.

I'll not turn back, whatever it may cost;
I'm called to live, to love and save the lost.
I'll not turn back, whatever it may cost;
I'm called to live, to love and save the lost.

If doors should close, then other doors will open,
The word of God can never be contained.
His love cannot be finally frustrated,
By narrow minds or prison bars restrained.

If tears should fall, if I am called to suffer,
If all I love men should deface, defame;
I'll not deny the One that I have followed
Nor be ashamed to bear my Master's name.

John Gowans

I really love this song.

I love that this song is personal. "Me," "my," "I've,"
"I'll," "I'm," "I." This song is not dealing with abstract
ideas, which may or may not affect the writer or the singer. This is not the kind of song that can be sung on be-

half of someone else. This is a personal statement, which the singer must own before she or he makes it known. Often I am drawn to hymns and worship choruses that use more communal language: "*We* Gather Together," "Now Thank *We* All Our God," "*We* Bow Down," "*Our* God Is an Awesome God," "*All* Hail the Power of Jesus' Name," and so on. This type of congregational singing serves an important purpose for the church, corporately and individually. We find common ground in singing great truths and seeking God's touch together, and we find comfort in knowing we're not alone when we, the Church (big "C") leave the church (little "c"). But when it comes right down to it, our relationship with Jesus is of the one-on-one variety. And as such, singing songs of adoration, confession, thanksgiving and supplication should be a personal, intimate experience—even while surrounded. Songs like "Take *My* Life and Let It Be," "*I* Love You, Lord," "*I* Need Thee Every Hour," "Be Thou *My* Vision," and this one from Gowans are crucial for anyone whose desire is to have a personal relationship with Jesus Christ.

I love that this song is sacrificial. There is talk of crosses coming, costly discipleship, servanthood, darkness on the path of duty, being despised, doors closing, narrow minds, prison bars, tears and suffering. Near the end of the 16th chapter of Matthew, we find Jesus talking with his disciples about his own sacrifice, his own death, his own resurrection. Peter, who in the previous passage had been commended by Jesus for giving the correct answer, gets it wrong by telling Jesus that these horrible things will never happen to him. However well-intentioned Peter is in wanting to shield Jesus from suffering and sacrifice, Jesus rebukes him for having earthly, instead of heavenly, concerns. Then Jesus adds: "*Whoever wants to be my disciple must deny themselves and take up their cross and follow me. For whoever wants to save their life will lose it, but whoever loses their life for me will find it. What good will it be for someone to gain the whole world, yet forfeit their soul? Or what can anyone give in exchange for their soul?"* (Matt. 16:24-26). It seems to me that great songs of sacrifice must cost the writer dearly. But those same songs can give the singers a glimpse of authentic discipleship, and the courage to count the cost, carry our cross, and not turn back!

I love that this song is missional. "I'm called to live, to love and save the lost." When John Gowans served as the international leader of The Salvation Army, long after he penned this song, he synthesized the mission of the movement down to three points: "Save Souls, Grow Saints, and Serve Suffering Humanity." He understood that a "salvation" army should be about the business of saving. His original lyric for the last line of this song's chorus was, "I'm goin' to live to seek and save the lost." It is apparent that Gowans was referring back to the words of Christ to Zacheaus: *"The Son of Man came to seek and to save the lost"* (Luke 19:10). If we are called to be like Jesus (and we are called to be like Jesus), then his lost-saving mission must be ours.

As I write this, the international community is searching for lost Malaysia Airlines Flight 370, and has been for many weeks. No one knows exactly what happened to the Boeing 777 or the 239 people aboard. We may never know. The search area is massive, and many experts believe the plane will not be found. But that doesn't dissuade the brave and brilliant women and men from all around the world who are joining forces and resources to find what is lost.

For them, it's personal. It's sacrificial. It's missional.

Is your search? Is your song?

PRAYER

Jesus, you are a lifesaver. You saved my life. Thank you for not turning back when your cross came. Thank you for suffering in my place. By your grace, keep me from gaining the world, but losing my soul. And, speaking of lost souls, please keep me on mission with you as you seek to save them. Amen.

God's Favorite Kid

When you come seeking Him, humbly in prayer
You'll have a miracle, He will be there!
For all who seek for Him surely will find
Christ, the forgiving One, gentle and kind.

When you come asking Him, if you're sincere
Don't be afraid of Him. Why should you fear?
For those who ask of Him surely receive
All that they need the most if they believe.

When you come knocking, He'll open the door.
All that was closed to you, He has in store.
Ask and you will receive, seek and you'll find
Food for the spirit and peace for the mind.

John Gowans

Stacy and I have three kids. We love them and we're very proud of them. If you're reading this and have kids of your own, I'm sure you love them and are proud of them. But our kids are the best. I'm sorry if that offends you. Let's not argue right now, but feel free to send me a note outlining all the reasons why you think your kids are better than mine. If you're reading this and you don't have kids, feel free to side with me on the "Who's got the best kids?" argument. Anyway, we've got three kids: Emily, Graham and Lauren. They arrived in that order, approximately two years apart. But when it comes to our love for them, it's a three-way tie. Hey, if Lauren can have more than one BFF, we can have three favorite kids. I'm not sure how it happens, but you think you love your first kid with everything you have, then another one comes into your life, and miraculously you have the same amount of love to offer.

Even though we love our kids equally, it doesn't necessarily follow that we treat them all the same. Why would we? They're wired differently. What one is interested in may be of no interest to the other two. What those two are passionate about may bore the one to tears. They have different tastes in clothes, music, movies and food, and will most likely each choose their own distinct vocation. While they all agree that their parents are awesome (Did I mention how bright they are?), each of them relates and responds to us in his or her own, unique fashion.

One commonality they share is that all three of them like to get good gifts. It's just that they each have their own definition of what a good gift is. Graham would not like it if we gave all three of our kids gift cards for a shoe store. Emily wouldn't appreciate receiving comic books for Christmas. Lauren would feel slighted if we gave her concert tickets. Because of this, Stacy and I select every birthday present and every Christmas gift with great care, taking into consideration the distinct differences of each of our children. We know them. We love them. We want to give them good gifts. Most parents do the same for their kids.

Near the end of what has come to be known as the Sermon on the Mount, in Matthew's gospel, Jesus talks about gift-giving. He has already described for those listening what a blessed life looks like; called for tastier salt and brighter lights; taught on murder, adultery and divorce; requested "yes" or "no" answers; discouraged eye and tooth trading; challenged us to go beyond neighborly love to enemy love; established a standard for humility in giving, praying and fasting; beat Dylan to the "gotta serve somebody" line; pointed out the futility of worrying about anything; and exposed the hypocrisy of any one of us giving another one of us an eye exam. In verse seven of chapter seven Jesus speaks of asking, seeking and knocking. He continues in verse eight, telling his 1st and 21st century followers, *"Everyone who asks receives; the one who seeks finds; and to the one who knocks, the door will be opened."* Gowans has taken inspiration from this invitation from Jesus, and has written three verses expressing the fantastic promises of Matthew 7:7-8. All who humbly ask, seek and knock will have a miracle; they will have their needs met, they will have food for the spirit and peace for the mind. And they will have all of this because they will have "Christ, the forgiving One, gentle and kind," and "He'll open the door," offering all that "He has in store." And why wouldn't he? We've already established that good parents give good gifts to the kids they love. They wouldn't give a kid a rock if the kid asked for bread, or a snake if the kid asked for a fish (Matt. 7:9-10). Good parents don't give comic books to a kid who asked for shoes.

Commenting on the Beatitudes, G.K. Chesterton observed that the Jesus way looks upside down to us because we are standing on our heads. This wisdom could apply to Matthew 7:7-8 as well. Asking, seeking and knocking may not be as popular in our culture as demanding, screaming, and breaking in, but that's how our awesome Father wants us to come to him. That's how he wants us to ask for all he has for us.

What miracle do you need to ask for right now? What or whom are you seeking? What door do you need opened?

Ask. Seek. Knock. You have nothing to fear. You're God's favorite.

> *"If you, then, though you are evil, know how to give good gifts to your children, how much more will your Father in heaven give good gifts to those who ask him!"* (Matt. 7:11).

Creed

I believe that God the Father
Can be seen in God the Son,
In the gentleness of Jesus
Love for all the world is shown.
Though men crucify their Saviour,
And his tenderness rebuff,
God is love, the cross is saying,
Calvary is proof enough.

I believe in transformation,
God can change the hearts of men,
And refine the evil nature
Till it glows with grace again.
Others may reject the weakling,
I believe he can be strong,
To the family of Jesus
All God's children may belong.

In a world of shifting values,
There are standards that remain,
I believe that holy living
By God's grace we may attain.
All would hear the Holy Spirit
If they listen to his voice,
Every Christian may be Christlike
And in liberty rejoice.

All the promises of Jesus
Are unchanged in every way,
In my yesterdays I proved them,
I believe them for today.
Still God gives his willing servant
Full equipment for the task;
Power is found by those who seek it,
Grace is given to those who ask.

John Gowans

All the believers were together and had everything in common (Acts 2:44).

This song was commissioned for a 1971 gathering of Salvation Army officers (pastors) on spiritual retreat in Derbyshire, England. The theme of the retreat was "I Believe," and Gowans seems to have contemplated and created his own creed, based on his understanding of Scripture. The first line echoes the feel and format of the Apostles' Creed, "Credo in Deum Patrem omnipotentem, Creatorem caeli et terrae …"—wait, that's Latin. I didn't mean to leave most readers out (including myself). Here is a common worship version of the Apostles' Creed (in English):

I believe in God, the Father almighty,
creator of heaven and earth.
I believe in Jesus Christ, his only Son, our Lord,
who was conceived by the Holy Spirit,
born of the Virgin Mary,
suffered under Pontius Pilate,
was crucified, died, and was buried;
he descended to the dead.

On the third day he rose again;
he ascended into heaven,
he is seated at the right hand of the Father,
and he will come to judge the living and the dead.
I believe in the Holy Spirit,
the holy catholic Church,
the communion of saints,
the forgiveness of sins,
the resurrection of the body,
and the life everlasting.
Amen.

For centuries, followers of Jesus have been reciting these words—or words very similar to these words—in Catholic churches, in Protestant churches, in solitude, in unison, in ceremonies, in Latin, in English, and in countless other languages. For a Church that often seems (to believers and unbelievers alike) more divided than united, there is something audacious in believing in "the holy catholic [universal] Church." By assenting to this creed, one is saying—among many other things—that we're all in this together, and we all really can be the Church. We really can stay on message and on mission to love God and OTHERS in such a way as to play a small, but sacred role in the reconciliation of the created and the Creator.

And speaking of those other things, there is some important Biblical and doctrinal territory covered there: monotheism; the incarnation, crucifixion, resurrection, ascension and second coming of Christ; the Trinity; and our own salvation, resurrection and eternal life. Gowans has a similar list in his creed, but he gets a bit more personal. He emphasizes the gentle, tender love of Jesus in the first verse; the transforming, refining, inclusive love of God in the second verse; the joyous, holy, free life available for all who "hear the Holy Spirit" in the third verse; and the fourth verse speaks to the grace, power, and equipping that is given to all who are willing, all who seek, all who ask.

I have already referred to the writings of the late, great Brennan Manning, and I promise I will not do so again (in this chapter). But in his 1992 book *The Signature of Jesus*, I read a note found in the office of a young, martyred, Zimbabwean pastor, and it made a tremendous impact on me. I was compelled to reevaluate what my life stood for.

The note started with these words: "I'm part of the fellowship of the unashamed. I have the Holy Spirit power. The die has been cast. I have stepped over the line. The decision has been made— I'm a disciple of His. I won't look back, let up, slow down, back away, or be still. My past is redeemed, my present makes sense, my future is secure. I'm finished and done with low living, sight walking, smooth knees, colorless dreams, tamed visions, worldly talking, cheap giving, and dwarfed goals."

The note concluded with these words: "I won't give up, shut up, let up until I have stayed up, stored up, prayed up, paid up, preached up for the cause of Christ. I am a disciple of Jesus. I must go till he comes, give till I drop, preach till all know, and work till he stops me. And, when he does come for his own, he will have no problem recognizing me ... my banner will be clear!"

What is your banner? What is your creed? What is it that you believe?

The words of other Jesus followers (early Church leaders, British Generals, Zimbabwean pastors, etc.) can inspire and inform our own spiritual journey, but it seems to me that we, all of us, would benefit from creating our own creed, outlining what it is we believe the Scriptures say about God, what he did for us, and what he wants for and from us.

Maybe you want to take a few moments to start yours now. Need help? Here's a time-honored beginning: "Credo ...." (Oops, Latin again, according to Google Translate.)

I believe ....

The Coming Dawn

My day is almost gone.
I can't be sad.
Its well remembered glories
Make me glad.
I've loved, I've laughed,
I've sat me in the sun,
I've known frustration, true,
But so much fun!
And all the happiness
Along the way
Fills me with gratitude
At close of day.

And if the twilight falls
The day's not through.
The sun-set hours
Shall have their glory too!
The day is dying
But I shall not mourn
When I'm so certain
Of the coming dawn!

John Gowans

Do you ever catch yourself saying, "I don't know where the day has gone"? Chances are pretty good that you have said that or something similar on more than one occasion. What do we mean when we wonder where the day has gone? We, of course, are not asking the question in a literal sense. The day hasn't really gone anywhere it doesn't usually go. What we usually mean is something more like, "I still have stuff I want to do today, but the sun is not cooperating." We all know that each day contains 24 hours. True, most of us aren't as busy as Jack Bauer—with one day to save the world—but we still have stuff to do that's important to our little world. And the days sometimes fly by, leaving items on our to-do, to-see, to-buy, to-go lists un-done, un-seen, un-bought, un-gone. And leaving us wondering where the day has gone.

On one level, this little poem from the pen of John Gowans can be read as a kind of ode to a day well lived and well appreciated. Let's not underestimate the value of such an ode or such a day or such an appreciation. Living a day to its fullest is a rare occasion for many if not most of us. And the chances are slim of being in the moment and aware long enough to reflect on the good-ness of such a day. Days are important. A lot can happen in a day. On the first day, recorded in Genesis 1:3-5, God said, *"Let there be light," and there was light.* He saw that the light was good, and called it "day." After separating light and darkness and calling the darkness "night," God had apparently completed his to-create list for that day. A pretty good day, right?

There are also days when not much good happens at all. When I was a kid, I inherited some 45s from my older brothers and sisters who had left home. Among the Beatles, Monkees, and Neil Diamond hits was an old Cheech and Chong sketch involving a substitute teacher who is having trouble getting the attention of her students. When she finally does get their attention, she asks a young man in the front row to stand, state his name, and read his assigned essay entitled, "How I Spent My Summer Vacation." He admits he hasn't completed it yet, but she asks him to read what he has completed.

> Student: The first day of my vacation, I woke up. Then I went downtown to look for a job. Then I hung out in front of the drugstore. The second day of my summer vacation, I woke up. Then I went downtown to look for a job. Then I hung out in front of the drugstore. The third day of my summer vacation, I woke up ….
>
> Teacher: Uh, that's fine, young man.

That guy had several useless days in a row. Which can be played for laughs in a 70s comedy sketch, but isn't as funny played out in real life (if such a string of bad days can even be referred to as real life).

The twilight and sun-set hours Gowans looks forward to here are available to all of us, each day, for reflection. Not every day is good, or well spent. Some days are harder than others, and seem to spend us or at least leave us spent. But in that time of day the Ohio-based band Over The Rhine refers to as their "favorite time of light, just before the day kisses the night," we can take a moment (or several moments) to catch our breath, breathe, and begin to either assess the day, or look forward to the next (or both).

Today, we put together a bench swing for our back porch. I am hopeful that Stacy and I will get some serious mileage out of that thing in the coming days, relaxing and reflecting together during our favorite time of light. Although, where we live, we may have to settle for our favorite time of fog. Still, sitting on a porch swing with your lovin' one ain't a bad way to spend your twilight hours (or years, but we're not there yet).

I am typing (if you can call it that) this chapter on Holy Saturday. Yesterday was Good Friday, and tomorrow is Easter Sunday. Much has been written about this "in-between time" in the Christian faith's Holy Week observance. Is this when "he descended," as referred to in the Apostles' Creed? Is this the time those mysterious passages in 1 Peter (3:19 and 4:6) refer to? One thing is for certain: 21st century Jesus followers have quite an advantage over 1st century Jesus followers in that we know what will happen tomorrow. Sunrise! Resurrection! Life! Son rise!

This, I believe, is what Gowans was hopeful about in the final lines of his *Sunset* poem. Days die. Jesus died. We die. But, on our good days, we are certain of the coming dawn!

> *Brothers and sisters, we do not want you to be uninformed about those who sleep in death, so that you do not grieve like the rest of mankind, who have no hope. For we believe that Jesus died and rose again, and so we believe that God will bring with Jesus those who have fallen asleep in him* (1 Thess. 4:13-14).

A Case Against Mixed Messages

There is a message, a simple message,
And it's a message for us all;
There is a Saviour, and what a Saviour!
There is a Saviour for us all.

Let's look at Jesus, for he's the Saviour,
And he will answer when we call;
Let's look at Jesus, for he's the Saviour,
Yes, he's the Saviour for us all.

If you want pardon, then ask for pardon,
And God's own pardon shall be yours;
For those who seek him are sure to find him,
And none who seek him Christ ignores.

Though you have failed him, and how you've failed him!
Though you have failed him, God loves you;
The proof is Jesus, so look at Jesus,
And learn from Jesus God loves you.

John Gowans

What is the clearest message you have ever heard? Think about that for a moment. And don't confine your thoughts to the message(s) a preacher preached, when she or he really hit the proverbial nail on the proverbial head. I'm asking about any message that you have heard or received that came in clear and rang true.

Some clear messages from history (in no particular order) that come to my mind are:

- Martin Luther King Jr.'s "I Have a Dream" speech from 1963, when he called for an end to racism.
- Winston Churchill's "Never Give In" speech of 1941.
- President Reagan standing at the Berlin Wall in 1987, calling on Mr. Gorbachev to tear it down.
- Abraham Lincoln's 272 words uttered in 1863 in what is known as the Gettysburg Address.
- Rodney King's 1992 plea, "Can we all get along?"

Clear messages, right? However, even some quick research on each of these messages reveals that they aren't as clear as they seem.

- MLK's speech has come to be known as the "I Have a Dream" speech, but that powerful portion was not in his prepared text that day.
- Many people believe that Winston Churchill just stood at the podium of Harrow School in London, said "Never, ever, ever, ever, ever, ever, ever give up," and sat down. In reality, these words were just a portion of his speech, and he said, "Never ... give in," not "Never ... give up."
- Before Ronald Reagan said, "Mr. Gorbachev, tear down this wall," he said, "Mr. Gorbachev, open this gate." No one ever quotes that part of the message.
- Most Americans know of Lincoln's address at the dedication of the National Cemetery in Gettysburg. And as crystal clear, and short and sweet as it is, not many (including myself) have memo-

rized the short speech—something PBS and film-maker Ken Burns are hoping to change over at LearnTheAddress.org.

- Usually, Rodney King is misquoted as saying (during the 1992 L.A. riots), "Can't we all just get along?" or "Why can't we all just get along?" But he simply said, "Can we all get along?"

So, written and spoken messages, as clear as they may sound at the time, are not necessarily remembered, or at least not fully or accurately remembered. What about non-verbal messages?

- The message was clear to the world when we watched video of an unnamed man defiantly standing in front of a column of tanks during the Tiananmen Square protests of 1989.
- The message was clear to the world when Rosa Parks refused to give up her seat on a Montgomery, Alabama, bus in 1955.
- The message was clear to the world when 30 or so members of the Amish community attended the funeral of Charles Carl Roberts IV after he killed five Amish girls in a one-room schoolhouse in Pennsylvania in 2006.

Words have their place, and can prove to be powerful. But they run the risk of being misunderstood. There is also power in presence. And while it too can be misunderstood or misinterpreted, that is usually willful—a choice (i.e., a man standing in front of several tanks is foolish, not brave; a black woman in the 1950s South was breaking the law and provoking an angry response; simple religious people don't understand the severity of an evil act perpetrated on the most innocent of their community).

Still, these people and millions more throughout history spoke volumes without saying a word. Messages of peace, defiance, forgiveness, unity, hope and love have been clearly communicated by women, men, girls and boys who showed up and showed great bravery in doing what was right, whether or not it came naturally or easily.

In this Gowans song, he seems to be pleading with us to keep it simple. He also seems to be saying that the message that will save us is not a political plank, or a protest song, or propaganda of any kind, or even a program at a church. It's a person—the person of Jesus Christ to be more precise. Jesus is the Savior (the American English translation of Saviour) for us all. Jesus will answer when we call. Jesus makes "God's own pardon" possible. Jesus will be found by those who seek him. Jesus will not ignore us. And Jesus is the proof of God's faithful love for all of us failed followers. Now that's a great message!

A few questions for us to consider:

1. Is the message clear to us (you)? Have we (you) clearly understood our (your) need for a Savior, and the price Jesus paid to offer us (you) pardon?

2. Is our (your) life speaking clearly to OTHERS of this simple message, or are we (you) complicating things, by sending mixed messages?

3. Are we (you) *fixing our* (your) *eyes on Jesus, the pioneer and perfecter of faith* (Heb. 12:2a)?

Humbugs

You really ought
To deal with him,
For after all he's Yours!
He calls himself
Your servant
If You please!
He breaks up
Everything that's beautiful
And then,
With saintly smile,
He gets down on his knees!
His piety is painful,
He lays it on so thick.
His saintliness quite frankly
Is enough to make me sick!

I don't know how You stand him.
But then I too have flaws,
And I too have the insolence
To say that I am Yours!

John Gowans

I know, right? "His saintliness, quite frankly, is enough to make me sick!" isn't a sentence you would expect to read in a devotional book, is it? I mean, Christians shouldn't be made to feel sick merely by watching other Christians, should they? And even if they do feel a bit queasy now and then from witnessing another believer get it wrong again, certainly they should keep it to themselves, right? At the very least, they could just confess it in a prayer, or mention it to a few fellow Christians. There is no need to write it down in a poem, as a seemingly easy rhyme for "thick." Is there? Without over-spiritualizing this little poem, I would like to offer three reasons why I connect with it and, I would hazard a guess, you do as well.

1. **It is refreshingly honest.** Billy Joel sang about honesty being a "lonely word," but the very thing he needed to hear. I think most of us would agree. There is something freeing about hearing or reading something honest. In this case, Gowans pulls no punches in describing the way he feels when he sees another Jesus follower following poorly. It is painful. It makes him sick. If you've never had similar feelings in similar situations, you're either perfect or you're not paying attention. Can't you think of someone right now who you like being around partly because he or she speaks as frankly as Gowans does here? I sit at a table in a board room once a week. We talk about important things, but one element that keeps it interesting is the fact that one of my colleagues speaks her mind, freely. You never know what she'll say next, but you can bet that it will be what some (if not all) of us are thinking. If you are parenting, discipling or mentoring someone, don't always say what you're supposed to say or what they would expect you to say. Be honest. It will free them up to do the same.

2. **It is painfully true.** This light poem about someone else makes a quick U-turn and heads back in
the direction of the poet and reader. While honesty can be refreshing, and freeing, hypocrisy can be
putrid and devastating. One of the tracks on a new
EP from The Singing Company (a Chicago-based
band—find them and their music at thesinging-
company.com) I am currently (and constantly)
listening to is called "Seven Woes." It is a work inspired and informed by the 23rd chapter of Matthew's gospel, where we find Jesus giving some
harsh warnings against hypocrisy. Gowans seems
to have "woed" himself as he wrote this poem, because he goes right from, "I don't know how You
stand him," to, "But then I too have flaws." It is a
disturbing moment when a believer comes to the
realization that he or she is pointing out the prob-
lems of someone else, while ignoring his or her
own, but it beats the alternative by far. Not coming to that realization isn't just disturbing, it is
destructive. To realize that we are, all of us, failed
followers, to confess that we "too have flaws," is to
truly know that while the truth hurts, it also heals.

3. **It is whimsically hopeful.** After expressing his dis-
gust with a fellow Jesus follower who falls short,
then realizing he's got similar issues, Gowans clos-
es this prayer poem by claiming to be Christ's. His
finger pointing has been transformed into a one
way sign (which, incidentally, is also The Salvation Army salute—go ahead, Google it). He iden-
tifies with the sinner, but finds his identity in the
Savior. This reminds me of a story Jesus told in the
18th chapter of Luke's gospel. It was a story directed *to some who were confident of their own righteous-*

ness and looked down on everyone else (Luke 18:9). It was a story of two men, a tax collector and a Pharisee, who went to the temple to pray: *"The Pharisee stood by himself and prayed: 'God, I thank you that I am not like other people—robbers, evildoers, adulterers—or even like this tax collector. I fast twice a week and give a tenth of all I get.' But the tax collector stood at a distance. He would not even look up to heaven, but beat his breast and said, 'God, have mercy on me, a sinner.' I tell you that this man, rather than the other, went home justified before God. For all those who exalt themselves will be humbled, and those who humble themselves will be exalted"* (Luke 18:11-14). I read recently that writer Anne Lamott calls laughter "carbonated holiness." I love that definition. I believe it captures what John Gowans was going for here, in these 19 brief lines. After all, there is nothing funnier than seeing our own folly for what it is, and nothing holier than finding ourselves IN CHRIST.

PRAYER

Lord, have mercy on me, a sinner. Amen.

As the Saying Goes ...

Don't assume that God's dismissed you from his mind,
Don't assume that God's forgotten to be kind;
For no matter what you do, his love still follows you;
Don't think that you have left him far behind.

For his love remains the same,
He knows you by your name,
Don't think because you failed him he despairs;
For he gives to those who ask
His grace for every task,
God plans for you in love for he still cares.

Don't assume that God will plan for you no more,
Don't assume that there's no future to explore;
For your life he'll re-design, the pattern be divine;
Don't think that your repentance he'll ignore.

Don't assume you cannot give what he'll demand,
Don't assume that God condemns you out of hand;
For he gives to those who ask his grace for every task;
Don't think that God will fail to understand.

John Gowans

I'm not sure who the first person to say it was, but I'm sure they wish they would've registered for a trademark on the phrase. There are various ways of saying it (since it wasn't trademarked), but the adage goes something like: You know what happens when you assume—you make an "ass" out of "u" and "me." Just in case this is new for any readers, if you take the words in quotations in the last sentence and put them together, it spells the word "assume." Punny, right? Maybe it started out as a spelling aid for the word "assume," I'm not sure. But beyond the cleverness of its wordplay, or the possible practicality of its origin, I think it's the truth of it that gives this saying its sticking power. Most of us who have assumed have already proven (over and over) the time-honored truth of it.

When we assume, we presuppose something to be the case, without proof. Sometimes assuming can prove fairly harmless, as is the case when I assume my favorite Major League Baseball team—for anonymity's sake, I will refer to them here as the Seattle Mourners—will finally build a play-off contender team in the off season. When they fail to do so, the only one who really loses is me … and their other fans … and the team, of course, lots and lots of losing. (Although they're looking pretty good this season.) At other times, assuming is far from harmless. It can be, in fact, harm-full. Assuming can go poorly. Assuming can hurt feelings. Assuming can break hearts and break up relationships. Assuming can dash hopes and crush dreams. Assuming can start wars.

In this Gowans song, the ones who assume are the ones who misunderstand, miss out, and mislead. They misunderstand God to be one who has "dismissed" them "from his mind." They assume "that God's forgotten to be kind," that he will plan for them "no more," that God will condemn them "out of hand," and that he will "fail to understand." These people also misunderstand themselves. They assume that their dirty deeds will leave God in the dust. They assume they have no "future to explore," and that even their repentance won't do them any good. They assume that they won't be able to "give what he'll demand." And they assume that their own failure leaves the Creator of the universe in deep despair.

These same assuming people miss out on a whole lot more than a playoff spot or a pennant. They miss out on realizing that the love of God pursues them wherever they go. They miss out on a re-designed life, and the gift of "his grace for every task." And they miss out on the peace and comfort that accompanies the knowledge that "Someone Cares" for us, and is making loving plans for us.

Finally (and tragically), the assuming people to whom this song is addressed (u? me?) run the risk of misleading OTHERS to misunderstand and miss out. Often, as the maxim suggests, more than one person is caught in the fallout of assumption. This kind of assuming is not a victimless crime. With such a misunderstanding of God and his love for all creation, and after missing out on all that is included in knowing God through his son, Jesus, there is no way these people (u? me?) can avoid misleading those around them. Commenting on Frederick Buechner's book, *Secrets in the Dark—A Life of Sermons*, prophetic "imagineer" Walter Brueggemann wrote, "Buechner uses words with such transformative power that any comment on them is like the moon palely reflecting the sun." Similarly, the transformative power of Almighty God is such that if we don't experience it personally—and we will not, if we assume we can't because of either God's despair or our deeds (or both)—we will bring others down with us.

I don't want that for my life or for the lives of those I love or for those I don't know, but whom I know God loves. Am I safe in assuming you don't either?

PRAYER

I pray that out of his glorious riches he may strengthen
you with power through his Spirit in your inner being,

so that Christ may dwell in your hearts through faith. And I pray that you, being rooted and established in love, may have power, together with all the Lord's holy people, to grasp how wide and long and high and deep is the love of Christ, and to know this love that surpasses knowledge—that you may be filled to the measure of all the fullness of God. Now to him who is able to do immeasurably more than all we ask or imagine, according to his power that is at work within us, to him be glory in the church and in Christ Jesus throughout all generations, for ever and ever! Amen (Eph. 3:16-21).

Spirit-Soaked Gifts

Now the fruit of the Spirit is patience,
And the fruit of the Spirit is peace,
The fruit of the Spirit is gentleness
And joy that will never cease.

The gift of the Spirit is healing,
And hope for the darkest hour,
The gift of the Spirit is love, yes, love
And power, and power.

John Gowans

Why does fruitcake have such a bad rap? For those who aren't aware that it does, you'll have to trust me on this one—it does. This dessert cake made with chopped candied or dried fruit and nuts and spices (and sometimes soaked in spirits) is a popular gift at Christmas and New Year's Eve (over 2 million sold in 2012), but it is also a popular target for jokes. Why is that? It can't be that fruit doesn't belong in cake, otherwise strawberry shortcake and pineapple upside-down cake wouldn't be so popular. It can't be the nuts and spices, can it? Those sound like tasty ingredients for a cake. Is it the soaked in spirits element? I tend to doubt it. While I am a teetotaler (actually I prefer coffee), I can't deny that alcohol is popular in our society. I suppose it could be the shape. After all, some of us have very specific ideas about how cakes should look, and most fruitcakes look more like a loaf of bread (or a brick). On the other hand, I enjoy salmon cakes, and they don't look anything like a traditional cake. So what is it about this poor, much-maligned gift cake that has the potential to make the recipient feel as though the giver wants to end the friendship or relationship? Could it be the taste?

Here's where I confess that I am asking these questions because I really don't know the answers. I can't remember ever eating fruitcake. I've seen it, of course. I just don't know what all the fuss and fun-making is about. I will admit that the look of most fruitcakes does not appeal to me. Many that I've seen look like the baker scraped some of the gum off of Seattle's Post Alley gum wall, shaped it into a loaf, and baked it. Ew! Gross!

However, there was one fruitcake that I almost ate (but didn't). In the early 2000s, I went on a spiritual retreat, accompanied by two youth pastors with whom I served. We traveled the 40 miles or so from Portland, Oregon, to the farming community of Carlton, Oregon. Just over 2,000 people live in Carlton. I'm not sure if that includes the monks who live at the Our Lady of Guadalupe Trappist Abbey, but that was our destination. We were looking forward to a few days of solitude, Scripture, singing and silent meals. It was such a peaceful and meaningful time. Remembering and writing about it now makes me want to return. Someday I will. Before my visit to the Abbey, I didn't think about monks much. When I did think about them, I probably just imagined them praying, chanting and scribing with quills and inkwells. I was wrong. They do pray, of course. I don't remember any chanting, although that might have happened. Quills and inkwells were nowhere to be found. I looked. We were on retreat, but these monks were not. They are an industrious bunch. In addition to a bookbindery and winery services, the monks run a bakery (trappistbakery.com) where they produce and sell creamed honey, date-nut bread, and … wait for it … fruitcake. Their fruitcake looked good—nothing like baked gum that had been scraped from a Seattle wall. Still, I had been exposed to so much bad fruitcake press that I did not indulge.

At this point, the more impatient and/or inquiring readers may be wondering what fruitcakes and monks have to do with Gowans and this song. Good question. The answer, I'm afraid, is, "Not much." But if you have stayed with me this far into *Someone Cared*, that answer doesn't come as much of a shock to you. The way my brain is wired, one word or thought leads me to another, which leads me to another, and so on and so forth, until (one hopes) I come to a point and make some sense of it all. In the case of this song, the words that sent me all the way from Pacifica, California, to Carlton, Oregon, and back again today are "fruit" and "gift." This led me to thinking about the fact that fruitcake is usually given as a gift. This led me to ponder the plight of fruitcake, and how so many people talk about it behind its back. This made me think of the monks who, as one would expect from monks, are nice to fruitcake. In fact, they take great care to ensure that their product can be gifted to the friends and family members of those who purchase it. I'm sure they know that some of it is also re-gifted.

All of which leads me to this: All Jesus followers have been given gifts and fruit from God the Holy Spirit. In Scripture, the gifts of the Spirit can be found in Romans 12:6-8, 1 Corinthians 12:1-11 and 28, and Ephesians 4:11-16. (Some would add 1 Peter 4:10-11 and other passages as well. Look it all up.) The fruit of the Spirit are listed in Galatians 5:22-23, and include love, joy, peace, patience, kindness, goodness, faithfulness, gentleness and self-control. I won't go into an exhaustive exegesis on these passages, partly because it would make this chapter way too long, and partly because I wouldn't be able to pull it off. Instead, I'll just submit this on the subject of spiritual fruit and gifts:

1. There seems to be no indication in Scripture that the Spirit gives every gift to every believer. Instead, we are each given what God wants us to have, to use to the glory of God and for the good of OTHERS.

2. There is every indication in Scripture that the fruit of the Spirit should be evident in the life of every believer.

3. One (albeit overly simplistic) way to understand the relationship between the two is that the fruit is who we are in Jesus and the gifts are what we do for Jesus. The two should work together in tandem, to bring OTHERS into the kingdom of God and to build them up in the faith.

4. Neither the gifts nor the fruit should be revered more than the Spirit who gives them.

You might have already surmised that Gowans exercised a bit of poetic license in this little chorus. He didn't list all of the fruit and he included some gifts (hope, power and love) which a strict reading of Scripture would not include. Still, there is no doubt in my mind that he knew where the good gifts and the good fruit in his life came from. And his words and witness made it clear that he knew who he was in Jesus, and what he was to do for Jesus and for fellow Jesus followers. I am also convinced that, like many of the popular holiday gift cakes, he was Spirit-soaked.

Every good and perfect gift is from above, coming down from the Father of the heavenly lights, who does not change like shifting shadows (James 1:17).

#PrayForSPU

Out of my darkness God called me,
Out of the depth of my night,
Out of the shadows of sorrow,
Into the life of his light.

Out of my darkness he called me,
Out of my doubt, my despair,
Out of the wastes of my winter,
Into the spring of his care.

Out of my darkness he called me
Into his sunshining day,
Out of my gloom to his glory;
What could I do but obey?

Out of your darkness he calls you,
Out of your doubt, your despair,
Out of the wastes of your winter,
Into the spring of his care.

John Gowans

It's been a dark few days for the Birksfam. Our home is experiencing a shortage of laughter, not unlike the drought California is currently struggling through. Three days ago I got a call from our oldest daughter informing me that there had been a shooting at the university she attends. She was off campus at the time, and was safe and sound in her apartment with friends when she called. Still, as I'm sure you can imagine, I was filled with a sense of worry and fear for her, for her friends, and for her campus community. It's all a bit surreal. These tragedies happen—of course, I know that—but elsewhere, to other people. Nobody expects to receive a call like that, bringing the violence and the pain so much closer to home. Yesterday, Stacy flew to Seattle, Washington, to bring a little bit of home closer to our daughter.

Strangely, miraculously, thankfully, there have been a few bright spots in this dark time: live streaming prayer services; pictures on social media depicting SPU students holding onto each other as if they were holding onto God (which, in fact, they were); accounts of selfless, lifesaving bravery; outpourings of love and solidarity from other college campuses and churches of all kinds; homemade cookies handed to students by neighborhood children; and healing words written in campus dispatches from SPU President Dan Martin, Stamatis Vokos, Hannah Notess, Jeffrey Overstreet and others as that faith community prayed through the pain together. One ray of hope that broke through at just the right time for me was a Huffington Post article by Jack Levison, author of *Inspired: The Holy Spirit and the Mind of Faith* and one of our daughter's professors at SPU (and our son's Little League coach from back in the day). Here's an excerpt:

> I am dumbstruck, dope-slapped by the ambiguity of it all. The mixed-up jumble of existence we call life. Priscilla's spiritual director from our Chicago days, Jane Koonce, told her, "In consolation, remember desolation. In desolation, remember consolation." We do. We have. Both. For everything there is a season. A time to weep and a time to laugh. A time

to mourn and a time to dance. I understand the rhythm of this, the wisdom of it. Yet sometimes we have both, even when we're not sure which is which. Sometimes we weep and laugh at the same time. We mourn as we dance, dance as we mourn. Sometimes there is consolation during desolation, desolation during consolation.

I know this desolation, this darkness, will not last. As Crowder sings on his new album, "There's a sun coming up, in my soul, Lord, in my soul. I see the Light!" Peace will, ultimately, reign at our daughter's Seattle campus. Always welcome, laughter won't stay a stranger long in our home.

I am contemplating this Gowans song and this recent, terrible tragedy on Pentecost Sunday. Perfect! The second chapter of Acts tells us that Jesus' followers were all together in one place. Not long before that, there had been a brutal murder just outside of Jerusalem. Their friend had been killed. And while it is true (thank God) that he resurrected three days later, the reunion was short-lived, and he eventually left them. But before he left, he told them to wait—wait for the coming of a power that would turn them on in such a way as to light up the world. Then, suddenly, the wait was over. A violent wind invaded that "one place," tongues of fire rested on each of them, and they were all filled with the Holy Spirit and began to say things they didn't even know they had it in them to say (which, of course, they didn't, until they had *him* in them). After being accused of public drunkenness, Peter stood and offered his first preach (Acts 2:14-41), concluding with, "*Save yourselves from this corrupt generation.*" It occurred to me while rereading Acts 2 over and over again (and rewriting this paragraph over and over again) that the only answer to the sound of this world's violent outbursts is the sound, like a violent wind, of God's Spirit invading and indwelling followers of Jesus to help save OTHERS from this corrupt (and violent) generation.

I know the sentiment of this song, and of the Scripture verse that inspired it (below), is that we were all once in darkness, but were called into the wonderful light of God. But in a very real sense, it also applies to, and can prove helpful during, a *Dark Night of the Soul*, experienced not only by St. John of the Cross, but by Saints You and Me of the Cross, by downcast disciples, and by traumatized college campuses.

> *But you are a chosen people, a royal priesthood, a holy nation, God's special possession, that you may declare the praises of him who called you out of darkness into his wonderful light* (1 Pet. 2:9).

But nothing worth having
comes without some kind of fight.
Got to kick at the darkness
'til it bleeds daylight.
—Bruce Cockburn (singer-songwriter, member of
the Order of Canada)

Open Wide and Say "Aaaaall Are Welcome!"

We're such a fam'ly.
How we love each other!
A close knit unit,
Ev'ry man my brother!
Each fam'ly member feels
That he belongs.
He thinks like one of us,
He sings our songs.
But while it's snug and warm, Lord,
Here inside,
Help us to keep our circle
Open wide.

We close our doors
For comfort or for fear,
But holy huddles
Are not Your idea!

John Gowans

There is no them. There is no them.
There's only us. There's only us.
—U2 ("Invisible")

> There is no us or them—there's only folks
> that you do or don't understand.
> —Fiction Family ("God Badge")

Last night, many members of our family met at The Homestead near Sacramento, California. We don't really call it The Homestead, but I grew up on "Bonanza" and "The Big Valley," so I just threw that in there. My parents retired way back in the 1900s (1995 to be exact), after over 40 years of service to OTHERS as officers in The Salvation Army. We weren't all able to make it to their house last night. Our family has so many members that it takes an act of congress to assemble everyone. And, yes, that last line was meant to make a full-on reunion sound as implausible as it did. However, since my Southern brother from the same mother and his family were on a Cali vacation, those of us who could make it—made it. It was, as it usually is, LOUD! There was a lot of food and a lot of funny—two of the things my family excels in. While it had been awhile since many of us had seen each other, it wasn't at all awkward. Being together as a family felt … well, familiar. After all, we speak the same language, we share the same experiences, we know and laugh at (or groan at) the same inside jokes. Don't we, Joe? I won't lie, we don't agree on everything. But we're all aware of those things and tend to avoid those topics, at least when everyone is together. I'm sure your family has a similar system. That's the thing with families. They know each other. They "get" each other. Even if they haven't forgiven each other for everything, they are still sometimes (somehow) willing to table grievances in favor of sitting at the same table.

Churches can be like that as well, which sounds good at first hearing. However, we need to be mindful that while we sing, "I'm so glad I'm a part of the family of God," there are usually those present who aren't. And, if there aren't those present who aren't part of the family of God, it could be argued (convincingly, I think) that our worship services are merely family reunions, where everyone present knows the lingo, the inside jokes and the hot topics to avoid. Look at the congregation you worship with. (Some of you may need to look for a congregation to worship with.) See anyone you don't know? If not, if never, chances are good that you are attending a family reunion every week, where nobody is expecting anyone they don't already share a history and heritage with. This is troubling for a few reasons:

1. It doesn't sound like the church that Jesus was referring to when he said to Peter, *"This is the rock on which I will put together my church, a church so expansive with energy that not even the gates of hell will be able to keep it out"* (Matt. 16:18 MSG).

2. It doesn't sound like the church that James was referring to when he wrote, *Real religion, the kind that passes muster before God the Father, is this: Reach out to the homeless and loveless in their plight* (James 1:27 MSG).

3. It sounds more like the church that John Gowans referred to in the poem we're considering here. You know, the Church of the Holy Huddle, where the mottos are, "If You're Here Already—You're Already Blessed!" and "Take A Seat—We're Not Going Anywhere."

I remember reading in Rick Warren's book, *The Purpose Driven Church*, that the congregation that doesn't want to grow is really saying to their community, "You can go to hell!" Harsh? Yep, and spot-on in my book (well, in his book—well, both actually, I guess).

So, let's bring it a little closer to home, because it is easy to talk about what a particular church should do, how it should act. What about us as individuals? Are we spending any time with anyone who thinks differently than us, talks differently than us, and/or worships differently than us? Or have we secluded ourselves safely—all "snug and warm"—in an "us" and "them" outlook on life? This way of thinking says, "I have the right to believe that I am right, and it would be wrong to associate, much less work with, anyone I believe to be wrong." We do have those rights, of course, but is that the right or wrong way to live? Wrong, I think. I also think I am a recovering exclusionist.

For the last few years, I have had the honor of serving on the board of directors for the San Francisco Interfaith Council, where Buddhists and Baptists, Muslims and Mormons, Presbyterians and people from a variety of other faith traditions come together—not to argue, but to agree. We don't agree on many doctrinal points (in fact, we don't even discuss them) but we are in full agreement when it comes to taking care of the poor, sheltering the homeless, feeding the hungry, standing together against injustice, praying for peace, and a host of other important issues. Serving with, strategizing with, sitting in silent prayer with these people has taught me the value of Gowans' prayer that the Lord would "Help us to keep our circle open wide."

So, Christians, let's be who we are meant to be! Let's be the Church! Let's get out more! Let's not shy away from sharing the good news of the gospel with OTHERS or from working with OTHERS of different faith traditions (or no faith traditions) to accomplish good things for the communities in which God has placed us. We are the family of God, but we would do well to remember that we didn't start this family. We were adopted in, by grace.

Jesus said, "'Love the Lord your God with all your passion and prayer and intelligence.' This is the most important, the first on any list. But there is a second to set alongside it: 'Love others as well as you love yourself.' These two commands are pegs; everything in God's Law and the Prophets hangs from them" (Matt. 22:37-40 MSG).

~~Lost~~ Saved in Translation

Let me be an interpreter
To make your message plain,
And turn men's thoughts
To higher things,
And better ways again.
And let my life
Translate the truth
That there's a God above
Whose nature can be best defined
As Love and Love and Love!

Oh men are slow to comprehend
And sometimes deaf as well!
In language that they understand
Help me
Your truth
To tell!

John Gowans

On Saturday, July 6, 2013, I was at a spiritual retreat in Big Bear, California, with hundreds of other retreaters. It was there, during lunch, that I first heard of the tragic crash of Asiana Airlines Flight 214. The flight took off from Incheon International Airport, near Seoul, South Korea, and was bound for San Francisco International Airport (SFO). Over two-thirds of the passengers were Chinese or Korean. The significance of that fact will (hopefully) be made clear soon. Upon final approach into SFO, the landing gear and the tail of the Boeing 777 hit the seawall and skidded for a few thousand feet before coming to a rest. Not long after that, the plane was on fire. The crew and passengers quickly evacuated the plane via emergency slides. Of the 307 people on the flight, 181 were injured and three, tragically, died.

The Salvation Army has a long history of serving people in times of disaster. Our emergency disaster services (EDS) ministry works closely with local officials, the Red Cross and other entities to ensure the best possible, united response is offered to those in need of help. But here's the thing. We usually provide for basic needs and offer spiritual counseling at the scene of a disaster, and access is granted from the local fire or police departments. With such a highly visible event, and government officials from at least three countries involved, it wasn't immediately clear to our EDS director what was needed from us at SFO. Add in the tight security at any airport these days under normal circumstances, much less the more stringent policies that go into effect after an incident of this magnitude, and it became clear that we weren't going to be able to do what we would normally do during a disaster response effort.

Still, Major Wayne Froderberg called the local authorities and offered the assistance of The Salvation Army. The response he received was a polite version of, "Don't call us, we'll call you … maybe." Not long after he hung up from that call, his wife, Major Trish Froderberg, had an epiphany; "They are going to need translators," she told her husband. The two had been married long enough that Wayne knew to act on his wife's inspiration. He called the local authorities again, and offered the services of Korean and Chinese-speaking soldiers and officers of The Salvation Army. Not long after hanging up from that call, the phone rang. Soon, just a few hours after the horrific crash, several Chinese-American and Korean-American uniformed Salvationists were being escorted through security at SFO and introduced to the survivors. Speaking in languages that the traumatized passengers could understand, this team was able to provide blankets, shoes, and much needed spiritual and emotional counseling. The Korean-speaking team was also instrumental in providing language support to airline, government and customs officials as the processing of passengers continued into the early hours of Sunday morning. A second team of Salvationists was dispatched to an area hospital to provide translation to passengers who were being treated there. In the days that followed, The Salvation Army was able to meet many of the physical and spiritual needs of the survivors. At the hotel where passengers from Flight 214 stayed, a clothing room was set up in order to provide brand-new shirts, pants, sweaters, underwear, sweatshirts, socks, basic hygiene items and even food specific to the tastes of the various cultures represented. We provided luggage too, as their luggage was still being processed after the crash.

Throughout the ordeal, translation played a crucial role in The Salvation Army's efforts to bring calm to a chaotic situation. Imagine going through something as terrifying as a plane crash in a country where the primary language was not your own. Now imagine someone speaking words of comfort and peace to you—words you could understand! Stacy and I were moved to tears as we walked around, witnessing first-hand the miraculous, selfless service taking place. My favorite moment was when Major Thomas Mui, who ministers in San Francisco's Chinatown, was asked to say a prayer for a large group of students who were finally able to return to China. I remember thanking God for the peace that must have brought to the hearts of those young people.

Listen, you may not speak more than one language. I don't. But we are still privileged with and wired for a translation ministry. Even if you don't have the spiritual gift of interpretation—as mentioned in 1 Corinthians—you have the opportunity and the honor to interpret for OTHERS. Every day, everywhere we go, there are thousands of people who are trying to make sense of life, struggle, tragedy, choices, responsibilities, mysteries, injustices, abuse, confusion, chaos, and the "pain that plagues creation," as the late, great singer-songwriter Mark Heard put it. They don't need all the answers. They just need a kind word, a wise word, a funny word, an encouraging word, God's Word spoken to them in a language they can comprehend. You and I can help them. We are them! We've been there, done that, and will eventually need someone (maybe the person we translate for) to help us make sense of it all again.

There are instances in the Gospels—Mark 9:31-32, Luke 9:44-45, Luke 18:31-34 to name a few—where followers of Jesus could not comprehend what Jesus was saying to them. They were either afraid to ask, or the meaning was hidden from them, or both. In the Scriptures cited here, Jesus was speaking of a gruesome death and a glorious resurrection. But it was pretty heady stuff, which his friends—his disciples—couldn't get their heads around. The hard stuff of life is hard to grasp. It can't be explained satisfactorily by bumper sticker theology. But if we make ourselves available to those experiencing the hard stuff; if we act wisely, but tenaciously, to get through or around the various security check points we're all so good at setting up around us; if we offer a hopeful word "in language that they understand" (spoken or unspoken) to someone in their day of distress, we can, by God's grace, meet people at their point of need. Some disasters, natural or personal, are unavoidable. But as Christians, our response should be compassionate and creative. May our lives "translate the truth"!

Ain't Gonna Study War No More

I'm not a man of peace
And quiet calm.
My fingers itch
To sound out the alarm.
To call to battle—
Mobilize the good,
And storm the forts of darkness!
Understood?

But I can see, O Lord,
That now and then
Great battles have been won
By quiet men
Who bring a sense of peace
And priestly poise:
Win battles with no bloodshed
And no noise!

John Gowans

PRAYER

"Lord, make me an instrument of Thy peace," prayed
Francis. And he was a saint! I know, I know, according
to your Word, O Lord, I'm a saint as well. But there are
moments when I don't feel so saintly. There are moments
when I come close to praying something like, "Lord, make
me an instrument of Thy anger, Thy justice, Thy vengeance,

Thy wrath, anything but Thy peace." Those prayers (Can they even be called prayers?) almost escape my lips when I hear that 300 Nigerian schoolgirls have been kidnaped by men with evil intent. When I read the statistics on human trafficking, when I see scenes (past and present) of violent prejudice, when I am made aware of atrocities against humanity in various parts of the world, these are times when, "Lord, make me an instrument of Thy peace" are not the first words that come to mind—not even close. Righteous anger, right? After all, there was that scene in the temple courts where righteous anger was demonstrated by your Son. And I'm your son, too. But if I'm being honest, I don't trust my ability to wield a whip well. And while I daydream about turning tables over in a righteous rage, I'm fairly certain the tables will be turned on me if those dreams ever come true. Another one of your saints—your sons—Dr. Martin Luther King Jr. wrote, "Darkness cannot drive out darkness; only light can do that." Lord knows—that is, you know—the world has enough bloodshed without me playing the vigilante, looking for eyes and teeth to extract as repayment for wrongs rendered. So, in the tradition of St. Francis, St. MLK Jr., and St. John Gowans, I will not turn a blind eye to injustice. I will, however, turn a cheek (Matt. 5:39).

Lord, make me an instrument of Thy peace. Amen.

Family Stores and a Hound Named Grace

You can't stop rain from falling down,
Prevent the sun from shining,
You can't stop spring from coming in,
Or winter from resigning,
Or still the waves or stay the winds,
Or keep the day from dawning,
You can't stop God from loving you,
His love is new each morning.

You can't stop ice from being cold,
You can't stop fire from burning.
Or hold the tide that's going out,
Delay its sure returning,
Or halt the progress of the years,
The flight of fame or fashion,
You can't stop God from loving you,
His nature is compassion.

You can't stop God from loving you
Though you may disobey him,
You can't stop God from loving you,
However you betray him;
From love like this no power on earth
The human heart can sever,
You can't stop God from loving you,
Not God—not now, nor ever.

John Gowans

One of the things The Salvation Army is known for in the United States is its thrift stores. Actually they are now called Family Stores, which is a good name for them for two reasons. The first reason is obvious, since mothers and fathers can find good quality, gently worn clothes for their families at a fraction of the retail price. The second reason may not be so obvious, but it's far more important than a good deal. Many of the women and men who work in the stores, on the trucks making the donation pick-ups, and behind the scenes preparing (sometimes repairing) items to be sold in the stores, are residents in The Salvation Army's adult rehabilitation centers (ARCs) for those battling alcohol and drug addiction. These men and women arrive at the Army's door from different avenues, but they share a dependence on some substance that has hindered their ability to keep their lives, and in many cases their families, together. Through a time-tested approach that includes counseling, work therapy, AA and NA meetings, chapel services, Bible studies and connection to local Salvation Army churches, the prayer is to return these men and women to their lives and in many cases their families. So, Family Stores make good sense. As The Salvation Army's satruck.org website states, "every donation and every purchase makes a life-changing difference. Not just for those in the grip of addiction, but for their families as well."

I have spent time with these good people. When I was a teenager, my parents served as Salvation Army officers in ARCs in Seattle and Los Angeles. I learned to play pool and ping pong from these brave people. In the 22 years my wife and I have served as Salvation Army officers, we have never been administrators at an ARC, but we have, on many occasions, worshipped, shared meals, studied Scripture, conversed, and just hung out with alcohol and/or drug addicted women and men. If you've known individuals in recovery (my only real experience is with those in Christian-based recovery programs) then you know that there can be something amazingly authentic about their spiritual journeys. They have been places to which they would rather not return. They are broken, but in all the right places. They know they are sinners, saved only by an amazing grace. Brennan Manning referred to it as "the relentless tenderness of Jesus." Manning himself was an alcoholic, and fully aware of his unworthiness. Still, he was even more fully aware of grace—not grace as a theological concept, but grace as a generous gift from a gracious God. The grace of God doesn't stay far off, waiting for requests. It's more mobile, more active, and more aggressive than that. Grace seeks to save! Grace is on the move. Grace goes to great lengths to rescue sinners from great depths.

English poet Francis Thompson (1859–1907) also knew about substance abuse, falling prey to the powers of laudanum, a concoction of opium and ethanol. In his seminal work, *The Hound of Heaven*, Thompson describes the pursuit of God on his soul. The poem begins with these lines:

I fled Him, down the nights and down the days;
I fled Him, down the arches of the years;
I fled Him, down the labyrinthine ways
Of my own mind; and in the midst of tears
I hid from Him, and under running laughter.

The poet is being pursued by grace throughout the piece, but is reluctant to pause from earthly pleasures long enough to be captured. In the end, the hound of heaven is far too persistent, and the poet surrenders. The race has been lost and the race has been won. The lost has been found. Grace abounds! Go grace!

Listen, I don't know you. Well, I may know some of you (and you may know some of me), but I don't know what you are battling. It could be an addiction of some sort. There could be something that you keep running toward, even though you know it's no good for you. Most of us, however, have a problem of running away from something (Some One, rather) we know is good for us. We're just not quite ready to be caught yet. So, we keep running. But the gracehound has us in his sights, and he is in hot pursuit. He won't give up or give in.

You can't stop God from loving you;
His love is new each morning.
You can't stop God from loving you;
His nature is compassion.
You can't stop God from loving you;
Not God—not now, nor ever.

So, the next time you are looking for a good deal, consider shopping at one of The Salvation Army's Family Stores. While you're there, allow yourself to be reminded of the women and men of the Army's ARCs. They are not only working to get you a good deal, they are working (many of them trusting the work of Jesus and the Holy Spirit) to get their lives together. And let them remind you to stop running, to give up, to be captured by grace, the hound of heaven.

PRAYER
Now all glory to God, who is able to keep you from falling away and will bring you with great joy into his glorious presence without a single fault. All glory to him who alone is God, our Savior through Jesus Christ our Lord. All glory, majesty, power, and authority are his before all time, and in the present, and beyond all time! Amen (Jude vv. 24-25).

Out of Shape?

I want to teach,
I want to preach,
To reach a soul for You,
And lead him to
The truth I know,
Because I've proved
It's true!
Be he a rich man,
Poor man, thief,
Let me lead someone
To belief!

The truth I know
I want to sow,
See grow in someone's soul
Until it bears the harvest
That will make
That person whole.
Delightful person
Undefiled,
As wholesome as
A little child!

John Gowans

The other day, I was at the gym. Yes, this is an author's
not-so-subtle way of letting a reader know that he or she

(he in this case) works out. The beauty and the façade of it all is that you have no idea how often said author works out. You only know he or she (again, he in this case) worked out the other day. Actually, as I just reread my first sentence, I realize even that point is not evident. All we really know (if we believe me) is that I was at the gym the other day. I haven't mentioned anything about actually working out, which leads nicely into what I am going to attempt to say in this little piece, inspired by this little Gowans poem.

The other day I was at the gym ... working out. It was early on a Sunday morning. Stacy and I were looking forward to spending the last day of our vacation by worshiping with a church in the Mission District of San Francisco, then picking up a sandwich and enjoying an outdoor concert. But before all this would happen (and it did happen, and it was all awesome) I was at the gym ... working out.

For some reason, I started comparing the gym to the church. It's not because the fitness center where I am a member (I probably shouldn't name it; let's just say it stays open 24 hours.) looks like a church, although the word pew is appropriate in relation to most gyms. Church was just on my brain. God only knows why I think the things I think, in the way I think them. And not only does God only know, but I sometimes suspect he's in on it. Anyway, I started to make a mental list (I was on the elliptical, so I didn't have enough breath to actually speak the list) of all the ways in which the church should not be similar to a fitness center (but often is):

- Members enjoying the benefits available to members only
- Dressing appropriately for the occasion in order to fit in

- Entering in the hopes of feeling better about ourselves when we leave
- Lifting heavy weights in the hopes of becoming more powerful
- Relying on motivational messages for our motivation
- Comparing our progress (or lack thereof) to the progress (or lack thereof) of others
- Stair climbing
- Way too much emphasis on the outward appearance (when the Lord looks at the heart)
- Going through the motions without actually getting anywhere
- Nodding our heads to middle of the road music none of us can agree on or (Worse?) tuning-in to our personal preference and shutting-out everyone else, all the while cranking-up the resistance levels
- Way too much emphasis on effort
- Spinning our wheels, but remaining stationary
- Equipping ourselves with water and a towel, but keeping them to ourselves
- Leaving the place to live no differently

I concluded my list with a question and a prayer. This can't be what "working out" our salvation (Phil. 2:12-15) is supposed to look (or smell) like, can it? Lord, help us. Lord, help me! Amen.

I don't know if your (little "c") church resembles a fitness center for members hoping to change some habits more than it does a faith-full community of believers hoping to change the world, but I hope not. And if it does, what are you going to do about it? I do know that the (big "C") Church exists for all comers as a place where the serve, not the sweat, is highly valued; a place where strength is measured by how much weight we help someone else take off; a place where deep knee bends take on a whole new meaning; a place where the wordless groans aren't ours, but the Spirit's (Rom. 8:26) as we are interceded for; a place where everyone is aware that the really important workout is the work done outside the place; a place where all of the movement actually goes somewhere; a place where all of the biggest losers win big (Luke 9:24)! It's also a place where women, men, girls and boys are in training to, as John Gowans puts it, teach, preach, reach souls and lead them to the truth we know to be true, to lead OTHERS to belief that they may grow into wholesomeness and bear good fruit.

Is your (little "c") church out of shape? I hope not. And if it is, what are you going to do about it?

P.S. If you are ever at the gym AND working out, I suggest making a list of your own. It really helps the time go by quicker.

ARGOspel

We wonder why Christ came into the world
A helpless, homeless child;
We wonder why he tolerated men,
The tainted and defiled.
We wonder why! We wonder why!
The Son of God as man came down;
What does this signify?

He came to give us life in all its fullness,
He came to make the blind to see,
He came to banish death and doubt and darkness,
He came to set his people free.
He liberating love imparted,
He taught men once again to smile;
He came to bind the broken hearted,
And God and man to reconcile.
He came to give us life in all its fullness,
He came to make the blind to see,
He came to banish death and doubt and darkness,
He came to set his people free.
He came to set us free!

We wonder why Christ came into the world
And let men hurt him so,
We wonder why the Christ should have to die,
Does anybody know?
We wonder why! We wonder why!
The Son of God as man came down,
What does this signify?

John Gowans

In November 1979, a group of Iranian students took over the U.S. Embassy in Tehran and took 66 American citizens hostage. Most of those hostages remained in captivity for 444 days. I turned 12 six days into the ordeal, but I distinctly remember (and I am sure anyone my age or older does as well) the hostage crisis updates on the news every night. I didn't fully understand what was going on, I just knew that the networks all had scary music and a logo of a blindfolded hostage ready to roll at 6 and 11 p.m. I now know that in Iran and in Washington, D.C., both, there were all kinds of ideologies and political viewpoints regarding our country's foreign policies in the Middle East over the years that factored into the hostage taking, how it was viewed and how it was handled. I also now know that unrest and "unpeace" was nothing new for that region of the world. Still, as a kid it was kind of scary knowing that American citizens working in foreign lands could be free one moment and not the next. I can't imagine it was any different for adults. Captivity is scary.

The American government wasn't just waiting around for something good to happen to bring about an end to this crisis. They were assessing and planning. In April 1980, eight U.S. servicemen gave their lives in a rescue attempt that was aborted. Another rescue was planned and considered, but ultimately scrapped. Finally, on January 20, 1981, 52 American hostages were released (14 had been released within the first nine months of captivity). Not long after that, they were paraded through New York in a ticker tape parade. Home. Safe. Free. I remember the excitement surrounding the release and can still almost hear the collective sigh of relief from a grateful nation.

What I don't remember is the fact that the number of

hostages would have been 72 if six Americans hadn't been able to evade capture that day. Thanks to Canadian diplomats serving in Tehran, the six escapees were hidden and protected until the CIA came and flew them out in late January 1980. I didn't mean to imply that the CIA just flew in, scooped them up and flew them to freedom. It was a bit more complicated and creative than that. In order to pull off what came to be known as the "Canadian caper," the CIA created an elaborate ruse, which involved passing the six Americans off as a crew from Hollywood, sent to Iran to scout for an upcoming film called *Argo*. The cover story had to be believable, so phony posters and business cards were printed, strategic ads were placed, a Sunset Boulevard office was established, a Hollywood party was planned and all kinds of money was spent—all designed to save the lives of six people.

SPOILER ALERT: If you've seen the 2012 Ben Affleck film *Argo*, you know that it all ended well. If you haven't seen the film, but you have read the last sentence, you know that it all ended well.

I'm not naïve, so I am aware that Affleck & Co. embellished, exaggerated, elaborated and fictionalized on the way to their Best Picture win for *Argo*. That's show business, right? Still, the story is compelling and mostly true. In one scene, Tony Mendez, the rescuer, is confronted by one of the Americans needing rescue about the probability of the rescue plan succeeding:

Joe Stafford: You really believe your little story's gonna make a difference when there's a gun to our heads?

Tony Mendez: I think my story's the only thing between you and a gun to your head.

The *Argo* rescue story was hard to believe, but it was all they had. It's not a stretch to say that if the rescue story wasn't believed (by those needing rescue and those whose mission it was to stop them), the lives of all involved in the preposterous plot would be lost. It all sounds familiar, doesn't it? We've heard this story before. You might say it's an old, old story: People are in need of rescue—they're helpless. A free man puts his life on the line and comes up with a rescue plan which sounds crazy to some (even some praying for rescue). He disguises himself as one of the captives, and leads them to safety and freedom.

Wow, that *Argo* movie really is based on a true story!

In this chapter's Gowans song, there is a whole lot of wondering going on. It all centers on the Christ, *and why he became flesh and blood, and moved into the neighborhood* (John 1:14a MSG). "What does this signify?" the poet asks at the conclusion of each verse and on behalf of all who have wondered or still wonder about the wondrous rescue story of Jesus. There are several answers offered throughout, but the main point is repeated at the conclusion of the chorus: "He came to set his people free. He came to set us free!"

I don't know if you are "helpless, homeless" or both. Maybe you feel "tainted and defiled" due to your own hostage crisis. Everybody has one you know. We are all either released former hostages or bound, blindfolded, tied up and tortured current hostages. Which describes you? If you are on day 443 of captivity as you read this, there is no guarantee that your release will be negotiated tomorrow. However, if you believe the rescue story of Jesus, right now, He will, in essence, fly in, scoop you up and fly you to freedom. That is no ruse. That is no Hollywood production. That is the ARGOspel truth!

All of you, slave and free both, were once held hostage in a sinful society. Then a huge sum was paid out for your ransom. So please don't, out of old habit, slip back into being or doing what everyone else tells you. Friends, stay where you were called to be. God is there. Hold the high ground with him at your side (1 Cor. 7:23-24 MSG).

In the Stuff of Mankind

All the stars sang together
On that first Christmas Day,
And the stars are still singing:
Can you hear what they say?
Angels join in the chorus,
Maybe ten million strong.
Can you make out the meaning
And the sense of their song?

God is hidden no more,
He has spoken his mind;
Wrapped the gift of his love
In the stuff of mankind.
Now his nature is known:
God is love undefiled.
And his love is revealed in the face of a child!

Shepherds too come to wonder,
Moved to tears by the scene
Of a child in a manger:
What on earth can it mean?
And the wise come to worship,
Go away with great joy.
Have they learned a new lesson
From this new little boy?

John Gowans

Consider the scandal, a young girl unwed
The talk of her hometown, imagine what they said
But this girl saw angel, she believed what she heard
And though it would cost her, she received the Word
And He came for the unwed mothers
Guilt and shame, stained with tears
And He came to say, "Love one another"
And He came, God came near

Take a look at Joseph, for he was a good man
But he almost left her, he didn't understand
But this man saw angel, he believed what he heard
And in the City of David, he received the Word
And He came for the man with a burden
Heart of pain, filled with fear
And He came for the men this world's hurtin'
And He came, God came near

And He came for the young man who's dying alone
And for the woman with grey on her head
And He came for the rich man with 32 homes
And for the poor boy who only wants bread
And He came for the ones who don't care that He came
And for the losers who have ears to hear
And He came for the girl who believes that she's clean
And for the guilty man standin' right here
God came near

So as we celebrate Christmas, let the caroling start
But as you're searching for bargains, take a look from your heart
And if you see angels, don't forget what you've heard
Consider the Christ, child, and receive the Word

And He came for the slow and the clever
So be glad, be of good cheer
And He came for the "whosoever"
And He came, God came near

Lyrics: Rob Birks
Music: (You didn't hear it?) Brian Bearchell, Ron Pack, Dan &
Ann Ashe, Rob Birks

PRAYER
Dear Jesus, thank you so much for coming. Please come
again soon! Amen.

Smokey & the Miracles

All that you need is a miracle,
And all that you need can be yours,
All that you need is available
The moment you turn to the Lord.

John Gowans

Love is a miracle.
—Sara Groves

A week ago, on a beautiful San Francisco afternoon, Stacy
and I went to see and hear the perpetually cool Smokey Robinson on the first Sunday of the 77th annual Stern Grove Festival.
It was a free concert, which was good because while we heard
him really well, we could only see him from a huge distance.
R&B legend Patti Austin opened the show; what a powerful,
soulful voice she has at the age of 63! Eleven years her senior,
Mr. Robinson still has the silky-smooth voice that made him
famous when his group The Miracles hit the charts with "Shop
Around" in 1960. (Nope, Captain & Tennille didn't write that
one.) The Miracles were with Berry Gordy before Motown even
existed and Smokey made many hit records for the iconic De-
troit record label, both with The Miracles and throughout his
solo career. At this point, some of you may be thinking you
don't know that many Smokey Robinson songs. Think again.
His songwriting and his voice have woven their way into the
popular music fabric of America over the past 50 plus years:

"You've Really Got A Hold On Me" (1962), "My Girl" (1964), "The Way You Do the Things You Do" (1964), "The Tracks of My Tears" (1965), "I Second That Emotion" (1967), "The Tears of a Clown" (co-written with Stevie Wonder—1967), "Cruisin'" (1979), "Being With You" (1981), "Just To See Her" (1987), just to name a few. Since the man has over 4,000 songs to his credit, I will stop there. As you can imagine, with a cache of songs that impressive, the concert was fantastic (though some people's idea of an outdoor concert "on grass" is much different than mine).

Although Smokey left The Miracles in July 1972, the miracles didn't leave Smokey. In 1977 something amazing happened while he was sitting alone at home. In an interview for *Guideposts* in 2009, Smokey said, "I was upstairs looking at TV and I heard God's voice say to me, 'I want you to know my son, Jesus, and I want you to tell your friends.'" A few weeks later, he related that extraordinary experience to an actor friend of his. "That was when we both got saved and started our relationship with Jesus." Saved, but far from perfect, Smokey's life took some bad turns. After a marriage failed and the hits slowed down (for a while), he developed a drug addiction that slid from marijuana to cocaine to crack. In his 1989 autobiography, *Inside My Life*, Smokey describes the hell that his addiction to drugs had him living in. He couldn't recognize his reflection in the mirror. Crack nearly killed him. Thankfully, his actor friend and fellow Jesus-follower loved him enough to confront him and encourage him to seek help. Smokey accompanied his friend to a storefront church in East L.A. where a female faith-healer laid hands on him, prayed for his soul, prayed for his healing, prayed for a miracle. The prayer moved Smokey tremendously and caused him to cry for hours (enter "Tracks of My Tears" reference here). He left that place changed—miraculously changed.

I don't know if John Gowans was a Smokey fan or not. My

guess is yes. After all, they were both writing love songs in the same era, albeit different genres. But I can say with confidence that John Gowans was a fan of the miracles. He believed in them. He witnessed them. He wrote about them. He was one of them. This little chorus comes from a 1967 musical he wrote with John Larsson. It is sung by a young believer who is letting an unbelieving young man know that a miracle is available to him, just one good turn away—toward the Lord. And one good turn deserves another, right? So God says, "All that you need can be yours. All that you need is available." I have known people who desperately needed a miracle. I have known people who prayed for a miracle. I have known miracles. Let me introduce you to two of them.

Joy (not her real name) was a teenager when I met her. She was raised in a loving home by two friends of mine who love Jesus and follow him closely. We lived in the same West Coast city for a while, but things change, and in my line of work, so do addresses. A few years after we moved, I called her dad, just to chat and see how he was doing. He always makes me laugh. When he answered the phone, I most likely started right into some routine of inside jokes, but it didn't take me long to realize he wasn't in a joking mood. I'm slow, but I'm not dead. "I'm looking for Joy," he said. And then he went on to tell me a story that no father wants to hear, a story no father wants to tell. It was a story of running away from home. It was a story of bad influences. It was a story of bad choices. It was a sad, sad story. My friend wasn't looking for his daughter around his own neighborhood. He was looking for her on the streets of Los Angeles. He was sick with worry. I heard it in his voice.

Back in the 80s, the SoCal band Adam Again had a song called "She's Run," which included the lyric, "Has anyone seen my little girl? We only want her to come home. We only want to tell her how we feel." But this was now the mid-90s, and I doubt my friend knew that song. (He is a bit older than me.)

Anyway, this was no lyric for him, this was his life—his worst nightmare at the time I called him. Joy was eventually found and, at some point, she returned to my friend's home. When I saw her next, I could see that her life had been rough; her countenance had darkened. Still, a loving family, plus a determined girl, plus a God of grace often adds up to huge miracles. Not always, but often.

I saw Joy a few months ago at a Christian youth leaders' retreat. She is a new person. With a family of her own, a steady job and a kingdom ministry, Joy is quick to give God the glory for the miracle that is her life. By the way, on that same Adam Again album, there's a song called "Miracles," which includes the lyric, "God's love filled me, changed me inside out. And if that's not a miracle, tell me what it is. He did it for me. He did it for free. If you need to see some proof—that should be all you need." All that Joy and her parents needed was a miracle. Granted!

Bruce (not his real name) had battled alcohol addiction for years. Fallout from this battle included the end of a marriage and a hard distance between him and his kids. When I first met him, he had been through rehab and was doing pretty well. We served in ministry together for some time, and I was so thankful for his gifting and the sense of stability and peace he brought to any situation (and we had some situations in this particular ministry). Then something happened, and he relapsed. There was a song several years ago that described saints as sinners who fall down … and get up. Eventually, Bruce got up. A few years later, I was fortunate enough to minister alongside him again. And once again, what Bruce brought to the ministry table was invaluable. He and I were more than coworkers. We became good friends, brothers. Then one day, Bruce didn't show up for work. One day became two, three, four, until it became clear that he was not returning to work. I was really worried about him, as were his coworkers and friends. The search for Bruce was on!

The town in which we lived and worked had an old highway that hosted all the cheap motels. For the next few days, we searched each of those (at least we thought we did) and looked for Bruce on the streets—praying to find him and hoping against hope that we wouldn't get a call informing us that he had passed away. Eventually I did get a call, but it was Bruce on the other end of the line, asking me to pick him up at the only dive we hadn't searched. I wasn't prepared for the man I found. Bruce remembers apologizing to me and that I replied, "It is now part of our shared story of redemption and grace," or something to that effect. I just remember that I was filled with joy that he was alive and, well, not well—but alive! I wasn't sure what would happen next, but he always had a hungry heart for righteousness, high hopes for the future, and he always believed the promise. We were all countin' on a miracle.

Detox, rehab, work/ministry, a community of faith, a Master of Arts in christian ministry (with a major in counseling), restored relationships with family—all miracles! And he knows it full well. I'm so thankful for him and the testimony of his life. I know we are both looking forward to spending the glory days together.

> There are also many other signs and miracles which Jesus performed in the presence of the disciples which are not written in this book. But these are written (recorded) in order that you may believe that Jesus is the Christ (the Anointed One), the Son of God, and that through believing and cleaving to and trusting and relying upon Him you may have life through (in) His name [through Who He is] (John 20:30-31 AMP).

Smokey, Joy, Bruce, me, you—all miracles in need of miracles from the Miracle Worker.

"All that you need is a miracle!" I have two friends who have been diagnosed with stage IV cancer in recent years, and another who is attempting to welcome leukemia into her life as grace-fully as she welcomes in other former strangers. A few months ago, one friend's cancer miraculously disappeared. The doctors were stunned, but it didn't take God by surprise. We all rejoiced. The other two miracles have not yet been seen by human eyes, but we continue to pray for them, believing (Lord, help my unbelief—Mark 9:19-27) that whatever happens is God's best for my friends and his. "All that you need is available." I second that emotion.

PRAYER

Miracle Worker, I don't know what miracle my readers need.
However, since they are flesh and blood, living on planet
Earth, I'm assuming they need at least one or two (dozen)
miracles. I pray that at this very moment they turn to you, and
find all that they need. Thank you for turning water into wine,
storms into serenity, and loss into life. Amen.

Barbara Jean

If human hearts are often tender,
And human minds can pity know,
If human love is touched with splendor,
And human hands compassion show,

Then how much more shall God our Father
In love forgive, in love forgive!
Then how much more shall God our Father
Our wants supply, and none deny!

If sometimes men can live for others,
And sometimes give where gifts are spurned,
If sometimes treat their foes as brothers,
And love where love is not returned,

If men will often share their gladness,
If men respond when children cry,
If men can feel each other's sadness,
Each other's tears attempt to dry,

John Gowans

My sister was one of the kindest, funniest and most generous people I've ever known. She could also be stubborn,
melancholy and difficult. Like all of us, Barbara was complicated, not easily labeled or categorized. The term "walking
contradiction" is too strong to be applied to her (unless, of

course, it describes us all), but she had her share: GRACE-ious/judgmental, vivacious/brooding, merciful/unforgiv-ing, compassionate/harsh, Biblical/not-so-much, and so on. Even while creating that short list, I realized I could have been describing myself to someone. And that is true not just because we are related. Our contradictions weren't passed on to us by our parents. I guess it's always en vogue for one to blame mom and dad for one's faults, but I don't believe our contradictions are a part of our DNA (which I just now realized is an anagram of our Dad's first name—hint: it starts with a D). A deep appreciation for music, a fondness for fried dough, the desire to make people laugh, these are all traits that Barbara and I and my other siblings were either born with or instilled with at a very young age. Inconsisten-cies in how we live out our faith (i.e., the correlation between our "talk" and our "walk" not being easily recognizable) are part of the human condition, a fallen humanity. So, even though you and I may not be related, we share a penchant for missing the mark as well as a capacity for contradictions. *Yes, all have sinned; all fall short of God's glorious ideal* (Rom. 3:23 TLB).*

This is getting too heavy, so let's go back to the beginning (of this chapter, not to Genesis, although in a way we were just there). I began by listing a few of my favorite attributes of my sister Barbara. To illustrate those, here are just a few of the memories I have of her:

For a laugh (several actually), Barbara used to tell people that her siblings' names (Dana, Cathy, David, John, Brian and Robert) all meant something along the lines of "gift of God" or "beautiful gift," but that her name meant "barbar-ian." I have since checked, and while Barbara and barbar-ian do share the same root, Barbara really means "stranger; foreigner; traveler from a foreign land." Oh, that fact might not have made her feel any better. She also used to crack me up when she would say, "Honesty is my policy." It was usually just before or just after she lied through her teeth about something.

I can only speak for myself, of course, but Barbara was the best and most generous giver of gifts. The earliest gift I remember receiving from her was a chair made of cardboard, painted brown and covered with black faux fur. It was a high school project I think, but I got to keep it in my room for a long time. One Christmas, I was led by clues to our garage, where I found a pinball machine—not the little, feeble, cheap kind, but an actual full-sized pinball machine. So cool! In my pre-teen years, the walls of my room were covered in Queen posters (the British rock band, not the British monarch), most of them supplied by Barbara (to my parents' dismay?). In my early teen years, while living in Northern California, Barbara kept my record collection stocked with the latest albums: A Flock of Seagulls, Men At Work, The B-52s, Falco, Stray Cats, Soft Cell, Roxy Music and others I just can't remember right now (but I'll bet you can guess the decade). As I grew up, I came to understand that giving of her resources (be they many or few) before taking care of her own needs was definitely a hallmark of how she lived her life. Some would call that being generous to a fault. Maybe, but it beats the heck out of being a tightfisted miser. *"For if you give, you will get! Your gift will return to you in full and overflowing measure, pressed down, shaken together to make room for more, and running over. Whatever measure you use to give—large or small—will be used to measure what is given back to you"* (Luke 6:38 TLB).

My sister Barbara had a heart for the hurting, a compassion for the cut-off. When I was a kid, I would sometimes visit her for a few days at a time. On a few of those trips, she introduced me to her gay friends. We shared meals and laughs together. To my recollection, those were the first openly gay people I ever knew. At the time of my visits to my sister, society in general was even less tolerant of (and much less kind toward) homosexuals than society in general is today. But my sister Barbara loved her friends like Jesus loves them, unconditionally. They were, after all, her friends. They were a part of her life and she was a part of theirs. I think we would all agree that it is much harder to judge someone if you consider them a friend. At least it should be, right? Years later, while living near Eureka, California, Barbara became aware of a family of six living in a travel trailer by the levy. She visited them and brought hygiene items, Christmas gifts, blankets and food obtained through her Salvation Army contacts. Barbara helped another homeless family get into an apartment and the mother and children became members of The Salvation Army corps (a place for worship and service). Due in part to Barbara's friendship and care, the mother continued on to nursing school. *"Love your neighbor as much as you love yourself"* (Matt. 22:39 TLB).

I knew long before today that I would use this Gowans song to pay tribute to my sister Barbara. It is a song that acknowledges the tenderness, the pity, the splendor, the selflessness, the generosity, the love, the sympathy, the empathy and the compassionate care that humans can exhibit. There are a lot of "ifs" in this song, seven to be exact. But Gowans wasn't asking a question, he was making a point. For him, and for anyone paying attention to life and the world in which we are all living it, it is obvious that "human hearts are often" all of these things, and more. Barbara's heart sure was. So, since even members of a fallen humanity can be compassionate and generous, how much more compassionate and generous can and will God be? There is nothing iffy about God. No contradictions can be found in God. God's "talk" and God's "walk" are in perfect alignment. *But whatever is good and perfect comes to us from God, the Creator of all light, and he shines forever without change or shadow* (James 1:17 TLB).

My sister Barbara had a beautiful singing voice. In fact my other two sisters, Dana and Cathy, also have beautiful voices. At nearly every family reunion, the three have been cajoled into singing a song they have sung together for years, "Wings of Prayer" (a.k.a. "I'll Fly Away"). It is a song written by John W. Peterson, who also wrote "Heaven Came Down." Here is the first verse and chorus:

Troubles may fall
Like showers of rain
Leaving my soul
With heartache and pain
But I have a refuge
A blessed retreat
Wonderful prayer time
At the Savior's dear feet

I'll fly away
On the wings of prayer
I'll fly away
Leave my troubles and cares
Jesus is waiting
My burdens to share
I'll fly away
On the wings of prayer

On March 23, 2013, Barbara did fly away. Jesus *was* waiting for her, not to share her burdens, but to lift them once and for all eternity. No more troubles. No more heartache. No more pain. All replaced by a refuge, a blessed retreat found at her Savior's dear feet. Barbara's life was certainly not trouble-free. Some would say she brought some of the trouble on herself, through choices she made. Okay, granted. You and me both, right? I say she lived a broken life and did her best to follow hard after the *man of sorrows,* [who was] *acquainted with bitterest grief* (Isa. 53:3 TLB). Her life made a huge, important impression on my own life, on my kids' lives, and on the lives of countless OTHERS. Part of her legacy is her "human heart," which was "often tender," and her "human love," which was "touched with splendor." Another, flesh and blood part of her legacy are the two kids she raised alone (with some help from family). They have their whole lives ahead of them. Their personalities and attributes are their own—some inherited, some instilled, some independently acquired, all theirs. They will make their own choices, good and bad, as we all do. Their lives will, at times, convey contradictions, as all of our lives do at times. They are both loved, unconditionally, by "God our Father," who gave them life, gives them life, and gives them eternal life. I pray believing that their lives will leave an impression on this world similar to that of their mother's—indelible, and indescribable.

PRAYER

Lord, thank you for making me (and Barbara and all of us) so wonderfully complex! It is amazing to think about. *Your workmanship is marvelous—and how well I know it* (Ps. 139:14 TLB).

*All Scripture references in this chapter are taken from The Living Bible, because another memory I have of Barbara from back in the day is that she used *The Way: The Living Bible Illustrated*, published in the early 1970s by Tyndale House, and popular among "Jesus people" like my sister.

The Privilege is All Ours

To be like Jesus!
This hope possesses me,
In every thought and deed,
This is my aim, my creed;
To be like Jesus!
This hope possesses me,
His Spirit helping me,
Like Him I'll be.

John Gowans

*But just as he who called you is holy, so be holy in all
you do; for it is written: "Be holy, because I am holy"*
(1 Pet. 1:15-16).

Well, we've come to the end of *Someone Cared*. Thankfully,
we will never come to the end of Some One caring. In fact, it
is more than appropriate to end with this piece by Gowans.
This is a poetic prayer for purity—for Christlikeness. As mentioned in the foreword and introduction to this book, John
Gowans served as the General (international leader) of The
Salvation Army from 1999 to 2002. This movement is the
faith tradition in which I was brought up. Various church
history books and charts place the Army in various catego-
ries or subsections in the Christian Church: evangelical, social justice, even charismatic. In the grand scheme of things,
I don't really care where we're placed (in fact, part of me

likes the fact that even after the nearly 150 years since our inception, some don't know what to make of us or how to categorize us). But since you've twisted my arm for an opinion, I will confess that I think we should be placed smack dab in the Holiness tradition. Catherine and William Booth, co-founders of The Salvation Army, cut their preaching teeth on Holiness revivalists, writers and preachers such as Charles Wesley, Phoebe Palmer, James Caughey and William Bramwell (after whom they named their first child—thanks, Mr. Court). One of our early leaders, an American named Samuel Logan Brengle, wrote extensively on his experience and understanding of holiness. The titles of his books reveal his passion for all things purity—*Helps to Holiness, The Way of Holiness, When the Holy Ghost is Come, Heart Talks on Holiness,* just to name a few. The motto of our movement, blood and fire, is embroidered on our flag (and tattooed on the skin of a few of our soldiers!). Oh yeah, we're a Holiness Movement alright.

Like most Christian faith traditions and movements, The Salvation Army has a set of doctrines (statements of faith). Number 10 (out of 11) reads, "We believe that it is the privilege of all believers to be wholly sanctified, and that their whole spirit and soul and body may be preserved blameless unto the coming of our Lord Jesus Christ."

Those words weren't just made up. Most of them come straight from Scripture. Near the end of the apostle Paul's first letter to early Christians in Thessalonica, he wrote, *May God himself, the God of peace, sanctify you through and through. May your whole spirit, soul and body be kept blameless at the coming of our Lord Jesus Christ* (1 Thess. 5:23). It seems to me that if it was appropriate to pray believing that 1st century Christians would be empowered to live holy lives, it is more than appropriate to pray believing the same for 21st century Christians. So, we do. We believe the Bible teaches that justification is experienced at the point when one's life is turned over to Jesus. We also believe that sanctification is experienced in the lives of believers as they continue to allow the Spirit of God to grow them into Christlikeness. As the book that explains our doctrines puts it, "The same grace at work in our lives both saves and sanctifies." We do not believe that holy living is possible apart from God's holy help. 1 Thessalonians 5:23 begins with *May God himself*, and 1 Thessalonians 5:24 doubles down on the fact that holiness happens only with his help: *The one who calls you is faithful, and he will do it.*

This leads us back to this final Gowans lyric. I think the best definition of holiness is Christlikeness. I guess that's obvious, since I've used it a few times already in this chapter. It seems preposterous (and dangerous) for one to believe that coming to Christ is all there is—that there is no expectation to grow in him, to grow in the fruit of his Spirit, to grow in grace, to grow in holiness, to grow in Christlikeness (there I go again). It would be a bit like getting married, enjoying the wedding night, but ignoring your spouse for the rest of the relationship.

The first six lines of this chorus go hand-in-hand with 1 Thessalonians 5:23. They are all about the author's (and singer's and reader's) deep desire to be like Jesus—that their whole spirit, soul and body would look and love and live like Jesus. The seventh line holds the combination to Christlikeness: "His Spirit helping me."

Much more important than where my faith tradition (or yours) is placed in church history charts is where you and I place ourselves. Do we think we've arrived when we kneel and say the sinner's prayer? Do we think we can do as we please, knowing that we can seek and find forgiveness? Do we believe in holy living, but try to make it happen on our own strength? Or will we trust Jesus, possessed by a hope to be like him? And will we trust his Spirit to help us to holiness, to Christlikeness (that's the last one, I promise). With Paul, I pray that your whole spirit, soul and body be kept blameless at the coming of our Lord Jesus Christ. Some One cared for you enough to lay down his life and give you his Spirit in order for you to live life in the beauty of holiness. Some One still cares.

AFTERWORD

I want to be sure to thank Charlie Peacock for graciously providing the foreword for *Someone Cared*. I have closely followed his work since the early 80s, during the "hot night on Broadway" days in Sacramento, California (when Michael Roe was singin' "Do It For Love"). My own faith has been enriched as he has worked his out through artistic expression. I look forward to more of that, as he continues to create and to come alongside OTHERS in making meaningful music. Join his conversations on a "new, humble explicitness" at GodPeoplePlace.wordpress.com.

I also wish to thank those who have endorsed *Someone Cared*. Your generosity encourages me. I respect each of you, and your work and witness continue to speak good things into my life. My prayer is that the reciprocal nature of our relationships will continue to edify us and glorify our Creator.

Lastly (but not "leastly") thank YOU for contemplating with me the poetry of John Gowans. If any of the prose or prayers in these chapters have caused you to consider in a new light the unmerited, unconditional and unending love of God, I implore you to act on it—accept it, reaccept it, embrace it, re-embrace it—then, as Charlie suggested in this book's foreword, "Hit the streets." There are millions of OTHERS out there who are dying to know how much Someone Cares!

Rob Birks